Build Your HOUSE and SAVE

Andrew J. Salat

Order this book online at www.trafford.com
or email orders@trafford.com

Most Trafford titles are also available at major online book retailers.

Printed in the United States of America.

ISBN: 978-1-4669-9595-6 (sc)
ISBN: 978-1-4669-9596-3 (e)

Trafford rev. 05/28/2013

 www.trafford.com

North America & international
toll-free: 1 888 232 4444 (USA & Canada)
fax: 812 355 4082

DEDICATION

To my mother, Veronica Celko-Salat, who taught me,
Timid Souls seldom gain life's rewards.

IMPORTANT NOTICE TO READERS

This book was written to enlighten first time home-builders on the joys, and possible pitfalls of building a custom home. It is a sincere assessment by the author, who has built two homes—To explain the emotional aspects of doing it yourself. Buying the building site. Being his own contractor. Saving on materials, and his experience in all phases of building a wood-frame, and a concrete-block custom home.

Nor does this book give a step by step information to completely build a house. A person must use common sense in all phases of construction. Though the author had never built before, he researched the building industry by visiting many building sites, questioned workers about steel reinforced foundations, framing, concrete blocks, reinforced with steel, and the safe use of power tools.

The book foes give all information on building codes for all areas. The builder must check with their local building department for codes for all building phases.

The author, and publisher shall have neither liability or responsibility to any person(s) or group(s) with respect to any loss or damage caused, or alleged to have been caused directly or indirectly by the information provided in this book.

CONTENTS

CHAPTER ONE

THE FIRST BOLD STEP

From primeval times, humanity's goal has always been to have better dwellings. Be it a natural cave, or a few tree limbs leaned on a hillside, we sought shelter from the elements and security from the marauding beast.

In today's complex society we may envy these primitive people of an uncomplicated era, who lived in their leisurely unhurried way. How easy it might have been for them in their unpretentious daily existence. They had no need for apprehensive meeting with the banker, nor decisions to be made about a 15 or 30-year mortgage. Unnecessary too, were the embarrassing questions about finances and employer's references.

Imagining the above scenario, could we say, "Those were the good old days!" Certainly not! For these primitive people, not many days passed when their very existence was threatened, and critical choices were made just to survive. Life must have been difficult, and so were the ungainly dwelling conditions. Today, we simply adjust a thermostat for comforting warmth, or turn a faucet for a refreshing drink.

Our high-tech and somewhat plush homes of today may not be as easily acquired as those simple shelters of the past. But the comfort and security we enjoy could not have been imagined by our ancestors. Building materials are now so varied and durable that we can expect our home to last a lifetime and beyond. If built using concrete blocks, reinforced with steel, our homes can outlast the Parthenon.

Since we live in a highly competitive society, imagine being immortalized a thousand years from now, as a future tenant moves into your home, wondering who had built a monument to themselves?

We see today's dwellings more than protection from the elements and wild beasts. Because of our competitive lifestyles, our home is the only place on earth where we can completely sequester ourselves from society and its effect on our private lives. A place where a sense of security is miraculously amplified as we step over the threshold of our home.

Yet, to live comfortably today requires a substantial effort for most couples. Competitive attitudes of fellow workers and unrealistic demands of customers drain us of vitality and diminish our spirit. For me this changed drastically when I left my work at the Post Office and approached the threshold of our home. My spirits soared as I opened the door to the laughter of my children and the aroma of cooked food. In this homey scene, the welcoming arms of my caring spouse reassured me of a gratifying evening. The miracle of all this has again put me happily in control of my life. Perhaps, in our subconscious minds, this was the reason my wife, Anne and I chose to build our retirement home with the permanence of concrete and steel. Strangely, we later wondered why we had slept many nights with the front door wide open. Does this tell us that we do not want to be completely alone? As a unique species on our planet, is it possible that isolating ourselves from the society may not be that important? Some may have a real need to connect to the outside world and casually examine the mirrors of ourselves, improve each other, to evolve into the noble creatures we were meant to be.

Many people live in substandard dwellings or double up in apartments to avoid high rents. Those of us who can afford such rents are often preoccupied in trying out our wings in new careers and achieving a pecking order in our competitive society. We just cannot take the time build a home from scratch.

To say that a modern family home is easy to acquire is for many a fallacy. A young couple will need years to save for that first down payment. Depending on the area, it might be $8,000 to $15,000, plus up to $5,000 for loan costs. Unless a parent or relative helps, home ownership for some could be a long wait.

The same situation exists for those who want to buy a lot to build their own. Unless the seller subordinates his interest in the land, it must be owned and clear of debt before a bank construction loan is negotiated.

Wishful Thinking Won't Make It So

How often have you driven by a beautiful custom home, tastefully landscaped and wished that you could own such a place? You wonder what kind of job or profession the owners have to afford such a dwelling. You notice that the large setback of green lawn and lush foliage. The larger than usual side-yard sets it off from adjoining homes and gives it a feeling of individuality, as if the home exists just for those who occupy it.

The back yard may have a tall sycamore or maple tree, gently embracing the roof lines, adding permanence to the dwelling. As you sit in your car, you wonder if you can ever afford such a beautiful place to live in. For one to reach such a goal one must either be well educated, or make many sacrifices.

You return to your own neighborhood with that abject feeling; all the homes have a common look. The developer planted the same kind of tree in front of each, and the 30-foot setback varies about five feet, while side yard minimum is so close, that the roofs almost touch. To your dismay, your neighbor's large speedboat separates your driveways. Of course there are laws on parking of campers and boats, but should you report your neighbor?

For the average couple the ideal dwelling is not easy to come by. They may have to change priorities in budgets and lifestyles. New automobiles, boats and expensive European trips may have to wait.

Financial experts suggest we save at least 10% of our after tax-earnings. In our plastic-card economy, very few of us manage that. Some of us pay up to 19% interest on credit cards.

My wife and I had felt such frustration many times, and finally decided to build a custom home for our growing family. As one who grew up in a farming village, I wanted more than a tract home on a small lot. I wanted our children to be raised in a more relaxed country setting, away from city clamor.

CHAPTER TWO

THE HOME MARKET

When couples can afford housing, most take the easy route and buy a ready-built home. The tract developer usually helps with the loans and other paperwork which may stymie first-time buyers. Some may prefer older homes, ones that may present more of a challenge, at times reminding them of the old homestead.

Some areas in this country however, have no need for new-home construction. Economic conditions created by cheap overseas labor has caused many industries to shut down, and unemployment can cause a tremendous population shift. When we go east to visit parents, we see small steel towns with many homes vacant, some store-fronts boarded up, all because people had to move elsewhere for jobs.

The irony of all this is, during World War II these industrial areas provided America with material and expertise that helped to defeat our enemies, the very countries that now cause the closing of the factories and unemployment. That old saw still rings true: "For a country to get ahead in world economy, all is needed is to start a war with America. After they lose, the good Ole USA will help become a world economic power."

In these former steel-towns and their cataclysmic economies, only the retiree and the poor have an advantage in housing. Property values fall and the tax base is less of a burden, making home-ownership easier. Some can even afford to stay in the large home they already own, one in which they can close off a part to save on fuel. If extra income is needed, the unused rooms can be remodeled as an affordable rental.

In the Sun-belt states, the opposite may by true in the home market. Mild climates, light manufacturing, and high-tech industries attract people of all ages. This however, creates the need for new home construction which causes prices to skyrocket due to rising land values. In spite of this, retirees seeking that ideal lifestyle can make their homes there and enjoy their remaining years in less hostile climates. This will hinge on several factors: choice of location, financial status, and one's determination to make retirement dreams come true.

The 1990 Census Bureau figures showed several Northern industrial states losing population to the sunny South. States like, Illinois, Michigan, Ohio, and Pennsylvania, to such an extent that it will affect them politically; fewer congressional seats will mean less clout in Congress. Whereas, the South and states and on the west coast have gained House seats. Example, California now has a total 52 Congressmen after the 1992 elections. Texas gained three, and Florida four. This census trend also added one congressional seat to Arizona, Georgia, North Carolina, and Virginia.

This inflow of Americans to the warmer climates created unexpected problems. Local agencies were hardly prepared for the economic and social impact of some the homeless who chose to move there, burdening the welfare system.

Other problems exist in our temporary paradise of the sun. Affluent retirees from the north and northeast will not question a sudden price increase in homes and will pay whatever developers ask. This pushes land values to a level at which few people already living there can afford. Many California developers build larger and more prestigious homes because of increasing land cost. It is not realistic to build a $150,000 home on a $50,000 lot.

Many are surprised at Oregon and Washington unique gain in population. Young Californians, disenchanted with high cost of housing, and crowded freeways, are moving there by the thousands. Ironically, if enough of them move, the same conditions will exist in these green states: High cost of housing and impossible traffic conditions. Some in those states are unhappy with their new neighbors, prompting the newcomers to quickly replace their California auto plates.

When a move is desired, retirees face several problems in choosing a new location. To leave an area in which they grew up and where the children are settled, could be as traumatic, as could selling the "Ole family home. Yet, if a spouse suffers from arthritis or pulmonary symptoms, a more drier and a sunnier climate can help.

We've lived on the West Coast for years and are accustomed to its lifestyle enough to notice that people in sunny climates have a happy-go-lucky, even a more devil-may-care attitude, one which can enhance retirement living. Whenever we visit the east, we notice people's more somber attitude, and a marked difference in philosophies. My question: Is there such a thing as a regional personality?

Before a couple chooses a retirement area, they must consider many aspects, both environmental, and economic. Example: We often shop for mother when we visit Western Pennsylvania, and are somewhat shocked by higher prices in a supposedly economically-depressed area. Whereas, in California, where fresh vegetables, and fruits are grown, prices are lower. Canned goods and other staples appear to be less costly. And so are department stores more competitive than other parts of the country. Utilities and housing however, may vary a bit with the area you choose. Our water bills, combined with trash are over a $100 dollars a month.

Back to building a retirement home. With the end of the Cold War in the nineties, a sinful national debt prompted Congress to cut back in defense spending. The closing of many military bases, and downsizing of our aerospace industry had no doubt added to California's economic problems. Yet, I believe our state is blessed with a unique assemblage of people who will find ways to circumvent their present economic problems. Though we at times miss the changing seasons of the north, our many years in the Southwest have been a blessing which we wish to share with all of those who wish to migrate here.

Many of us made plans for that ultimate dream home, only to put it off because of finances or wrong timing. All this changes as we reach mid-life and are more sure-footed financially. Our decision making has improved, and our niche in society firmly established. Our brood is now old enough to leave, or has left the nest, and a chance to accumulate more funds is at hand. The next few years could be a good time to carefully plan our retirement strategy. Should we live in the home where the children grew up? Maybe the urge of starting a new life and dreams we had put on hold can now be fulfilled. It may now be possible to join those brave couples who actually take that bold step and buy a lot in the country, away from the noisy crowd, and high cost of living.

We enjoyed our La Habra Height's owner-built home, one our three children still talk about. Twelve years later, everything however, changed, when each went their way, and we were left alone. If we thought that was bad, right below our quiet community, a new shopping-center sprung up, and there went my night-sky, polluted with bright lights.

One evening, my sympathetic spouse found me by my telescope, in deep thought. "Sorry about the bright sky," Showing a conspiring mile, added, "But I wouldn't give up: This weekend we can a take drive in the country, far from city lights . . . ."

"Now you are talking!" I said, stopping her. "I know just the place: with a view to three counties, and many cities below."

Anne's smile turned into a frown. "You don't mean our drive on Ortega highway? Honey, a beautiful area, but so isolated."

"Exactly!" I eagerly replied. "Miles from city lights, a place where I can build an observatory, with a research-grade telescope."

Anne gives me this direct look, "Now I am worried,"

"But why?"

"Some years ago, you promised to build me a home, and we ended up with a two story mansion."

"And, so what? The sale of this place will allow us to build a retirement home, and save."

"A good point. Now, cross your heart, and promise when you build your telescope, it won't compete with the Palomar observatory?"

Happy as a Lark, I stood to embrace my comedienne. "Sweetheart! You should know that financially, a 200 inch mirror is out of the question."

Anne returned my hug, laughing. "Of course! But you usually get lost in so many hobbies, I'm never quite sure about you."

Before we built our La Habra home, we should have talked to people who had gone through all the building phases to avoid some of the pitfalls. Being young and impulsive with a "We want to do it ourselves" attitude, we bought an acre avocado-grove with a tiny cottage, one built years ago as a weekend retreat by the beach crowd.

Before buying, we explored the tot, and the many avocado trees, then walked up a grassy knoll, and to our surprise, discovered a view to Long Beach, and Catalina Island. I must be truthful and say, we kept mum about the fantastic view, and purchased the place for the listed price, (Baby-Boomers take notice) $11,500.

Sure our kids complained about the tiny little cottage we were forced to live in, Months later, when shown the preliminary plans I had drawn, they stopped their complaints. Young as they were, they imagined moving from a little shack, to a new 2,700 sq. ft. home, with threw baths. The best part, no more dancing the jig by the single bath we had, waiting for someone to finish.

Like most couples, we knew little about building a home from scratch. For a while I visited building sites, to see how to begin. Since my white-color job required me to wear a white shirt, I'd visit a building site with a writing pad in hand. No doubt, the workers took me for some minor department clerk, and easily replied to my questions. Important ones about grading, foundation, framing, and insulation. I also took time to visit a local building department people, for information about building codes, and asked if they would accept my drawings. They said, yes, as long as building codes were followed. One man even offered me old blueprints as a sample for me to follow.

A month later, I came into the Building and Safety office to have my drawings checked. The man examined the data on first sheet, and gave me a serious look. "You're building a 2,700 sq. ft. home, on a steep grade, and have never built before?"

I returned his hard look. "Would you build a small home on a lot, with a view to Catalina Island?"

He showed a stingy grin. "A good point. Give us a couple of days, to check the plans."

Of course, I had to redraw, and was asked to get a structural engineer to show how a second-story dining-room on steel stilts would be connected to the main structure. Because of our steep lot, we needed a contour map and grading plan from a civil engineer. We met with a structural engineer for valuable input on the six-foot retaining wall, which not only acted as a footing, but saved us time and money by keeping the downstairs dry during the rainy season.

Being a first time home builders, we had to open our minds to new building concepts, and suggestions from professionals which helped us much in building a safer and a more efficient home.

To the reader, the above may seem a lot of trouble, but when one considers the end results, the rewards are worth the effort. As first-time owner-builder, I was pleasantly surprised by the Building Department people's treatment. Knowing I was inexperienced, they were respectful, and eager to advise me in solving problems.

Our steep building-site however, was a big problem, which a friend described as impossible. We were lucky in hiring an experienced grading contractor, who said he'd seen owners, forced to use expensive concrete retaining walls, before starting construction. Since our property already had a tiny home, and a carport, we asked the city planning department if we could make it into a guest house, and build another on the higher elevation.

The planning clerk pulled a street map from a large bin, studied it for a while, and said, "You're lot is more than an acre, you can build another home. However, you must first submit preliminary drawings, showing location of proposed building site, and legal setbacks."

One must live this to know the feeling of elation we had with the decision to build our first home. We nearly danced through stores, buying up home magazines, and how-to books. To get design ideas, we visited our new neighborhood for home styles.

"There's a different home," I pointed as we drove, "Will you look at that beautiful lawn, with a circular drive?"

Anne too had a thought. "What I'd like in our master suite, is a dressing room.""Wonderful! We have much thinking, and planning ahead of us, which will be the best part of our home-building experience."

"Look there!" She said. "Now there is a home we could build."

"I glanced at the sprawling beauty, and frowned. "We could, but could we afford the property tax on such a place?"

We were like a couple of kids drifting on cloud nine to our personal fairyland. We had made a good purchase in La Habra Heights. The little house was a place to live, so there was no rush to build. We also found that buying a site with improvements, is ideal for first-time builders, and such a move can be profitable too. Our building would be much easier while living near the building site. And after the main home is completed, the guest house can be used for an aging parent, or a close relative. Since all our relatives lived back East, we rented the guest home to a lovely young couple, who enjoyed living close to nature. Results: No pain at tax-time.

To bring power to the building site, we used a heavy-duty three-wire extension cord. Another plus, with us living near the building site, we were accessible to subcontractors and had control of the delivery of building materials. With our presence, neither was theft a problem at our site. Yes, we did feel a bit cramped in the small home during construction. Our final reward; would be a delightful move into a brand new home whose size nearly overwhelmed us. A wonderful place built with pride as a family project.

Before the actual planning began, we wanted a feel of the new neighborhood, schools, and shopping centers. When that wore off, the floor plan and exterior elevations took priority. I changed the drawings many times as new ideas materialized. Our plan was to build that elusive perfect home;. What dreamers we were then? The size and location of each room, materials to be used and the style of the home was such an exciting challenge.

I wisely visited tract building sites, and took brochures to get ideas for floor-plans. Though our friends gave us more magazines for ideas, nothing was right for that first owner-built home. Especially one on a steep hill, with a nearly two-to-one grade, which added to the building cost.

But, we didn't care. Our small income from rentals would get us started. Our new home would be especially designed for our family, and our building site. And, except for grading, plumbing, and a ceramic tile contractors, we'd build the home ourselves.

I'd advise my reader to visit construction, sites for ideas, in the different phases of building. "The last you need is a missing finger," a job foreman warned. One can learn much by observing footings, framing, and roofing contractors at work. In my white shirt, and a clip-board in hand, I'd walk about, taking notes, The workers probably took me for a bureaucrat doing his tedious job. For me however, observing the different stages of construction, was not only enlightening, but helped me much in our own building. One should not overlook building suppliers for information; their advice and instructions were quite useful, often directing us to others for hard-to-find building materials.

A subscription to *Sky and Telescope* Magazine had me hooked on astronomy enough to plan an observatory on the third floor. While drawing the sliding roof plans, my loving spouse looked over my shoulder, and teased, "First it was cabinet-making, then electronic experimenting. Does the observatory mean, to get your attention, I now have to compete with heavenly objects?"

CHAPTER THREE

FINANCIAL PLANNING

The idea for this book took root several years after I retired, when we felt we've done it all, and reached a plateau where new challenges again intrigued us. We had done well as a seasoned couple, met most of our goals in our marriage. Since our modest real-estate investments made us feel financially comfortable, we and the children loved living in our first owner-built home.

I'm sure many parents experience a feeling of awe when their 18-year-old son. grew almost a head taller than they. Counting our blessings of good health, we still had many years left. Our family scrapbook became testimony to the many pleasures and excitement we experienced while planning and building the home we lived in, the choices made, and challenges we overcame.

As we leafed through the family picture albums, I thought; why not write about home-building? Our experience could be helpful to other future retirees. Especially those who live in two-story homes.

We had such fun building our first, the book could encourage others to do the same. Especially at the time in their lives, when challenges are needed. The second reason: Many our age will not be able to afford the property taxes on their larger homes.

Medical studies find the modern middle-aged couples are more health and leisure oriented. Also, high-tech medical procedures allow us to live longer, and take better care of ourselves. We saw bumper stickers on new campers and motor homes, read: "We're Spending Our Kid's inheritance."

We often volunteer in community affairs and sign up for night classes. Dean, a friend we know, has gone into part-time consulting after he retired. What better qualification can one have than having climbed the ladder as an executive in a top firm? Many companies now draw on this important part-time labor pool.

It was different 50 years ago. If he or she survived, a retiree was "sent out to pasture". For some, if good health permitted, traveled to break the monotony.

With the advent of high-tech medical drugs; most of us reach the 80s and beyond. Seniors should stay active, by starting new careers, or by volunteering for non-profit ionizations. I did that for several years as a pay-back for my exemplary life.

Some people sadly discover when nearing retirement age, that Social Security will not sustain a comfortable lifestyle. Even if they are debt-free and their home paid for, a small financial crisis will throw them into a stressful tailspin.

We are hearing persisting doubts about the future of Social Security. After the Baby-boomers start drawing from it, will there be enough workers to support it? We must view all aspects of this problem when planning for the happy and worry-free days of retirement.

Presently, about 30 per cent of American workers have company sponsored retirement plans, prompting more individuals to do-it-yourself retirement planning. Today's workers must take a bigger responsibility in their future planning then their parents before them, as corporation mergers, and change in new company policies are less concerned about retirement funds, than how to compete in a more open world economy.

In our productive years, most of us try to build a retirement annuity with payroll deductions to IRA, or other employer sponsored tax free plans. If health costs are a worry, Medicare pays 80%, and we can join a supplementary plan to cover the balance. We can set up a health-plan to make sure we enjoy the golden years without stress, or the nagging possibility of an e illness-related debt which can bankrupt us.

How we determine the size of our retirement income will depend on $75,000 a year, we may now find it hard to adjust to $25,000. We will have to plan for a large investment portfolio to support our spending habits of the past, by adjusting to simpler lifestyles.

As an example, a couple had been living modestly on $50,000 a year income. At retirement, their needs are less, and they may easily do well with $36,000. They will need an extra $18,000 a year to supplement their estimated $18,000 in Social Security.

To get the extra $18,000, a minimum of $300,000 in retirement investments are needed. With present low interest the banks pay, the $18,000 Social Security will bring their total income to $36,000. This may appear adequate for most, but there is a fly in the ointment; a persistent inflation which has plagued our economy for years. Example: If we figure inflation rate at only five percent per year, in ten years the value of the $300,000 investment will decrease by 50 percent. This will further lower a retiree's standard of living and cause havoc in the slightest financial crisis. The immediate solution is to aim high in our retirement strategy while still actively employed. Don't look at past performance of our economy and rate of inflation. It would be prudent to put off buying that luxury automobile as a reward of your career success. Put the money instead into a favorite growth mutual fund, or the more secure Treasury bills.

Let us say we are now in our 50s, enjoying life to the fullest, and promoted to top salaries in our careers. We finally bought that luxury automobile we had so much admired. It is so comfortable knowing what we are going to do today, next week, or next year.

We are entrenched in this idea of coasting through life with this safety net of knowledge and security. Nothing will jolt us out of it, not even the occasional thought of retirement in a couple of years. Haven't we worked long and hard to fulfill the American Dream? Let's not rock the boat of complacency. After all, we earned the right to this luxury boat ride, we tell ourselves.

This was our attitude at the time and it was wrong. With life expectancy increasing, many of us will work until 70 to enhance our retirement years. Unless we have a rich relative, planning early in our fifties would be a wise move. To follow the old adage: make hay while the sun shines is still good advice. Seldom can we predict future economic growth, and those that can, draw top salaries on Wall Street.

The Party

Several years ago we attended a retirement party honoring a fellow worker. This type of gathering usually brings out several speeches, along with amusing anecdotes about retirement. In this jolly mood, someone asked our friends where they planned to live in retirement. Reluctantly our guest of honor stood up, "Helen and I plan to sell our home, and move to Oregon. We have already found a place."

The party took on a more serious note after his surprising statement, and the glow from my favorite wine slowly faded with the sobering thought of our own retirement.

"What do you think?" I asked my spouse. "Will our retirement income allow us to live in our present home, or must we move to another state for more affordable housing?"

"Oh, I like Oregon," She said. "It's a lovely green state with many good qualities. But our children will be five-hundred miles away, and so will our future grandchildren."

A vague cloud came over the party, and as conversation subdued, we said good-bye, wishing luck to our friends in their retirement. At home, we made the decision to remain in California.

"To be truthful, before this evening retirement was a most distant thought from my mind," I said. "See what happens when we attend parties?"

"If I know my husband, he'll find a way to stay in California." replied my confident spouse. The questions we asked ourselves were a little different this time. Soon we would experience that "empty nest" feeling. When we built our first home some years ago, we needed more space for our growing children. Our desire then was to find a more country-like setting, perhaps an acre or two, where the children could build a tree house or ride a skate board without complaints from neighbors. We could see a long driveway for safe skateboarding and go-carts.

"Daddy, do you think I could have a horse now that we have more land?" our daughter Joan asked. Later, the look on her face was reward enough, when I finished the stall for her mare Tammy.

Our needs were quite different then. Now the children are grown and would go their own ways, some to college, others learning a trade. The years in our new home in La Habra Heights were enjoyable for them. Scouting, horseback riding, and supervised cave digging were activities that will stay with them always. We admired their suntanned bodies running up and down those steep hills as they developed into strong and healthy teenagers.

Our area had grown, with new homes going up everywhere. Vacant lots were busy with carpenters building forms for new foundations. Some owners wanted to split the land into half acres, but strong opposition from the majority wanted to keep the acre at the minimum.

Other changes were more on the negative side. Los Angeles County continued to raise property taxes like there was no tomorrow. We felt that the county government had a bottomless pit called the treasury, and the best way to fill it was to tax the property owners out of existence. At first we thought our county was the only one with its unappeased appetite for money. A few years later, a couple of honest gentlemen in Sacramento saw that most Californians suffered the same fate, and introduced the now famous Proposition 13.

We never saw such support for a bill in California. The property owners joined together and passed it by an impressive margin.

Now the county property tax is limited to about one-and-quarter percent of the home value. Older people on limited incomes could keep their homes without borrowing to pay taxes. Young couples could qualify for their first home with more ease because of Proposition 13.

The Subject of Retirement

The subject of retirement came up more frequently after the party. Our after-dinner talks brought up important questions needing answers.

"We have many years before I retire, honey." I said. "Why the rush? We love La Habra Heights, close to everything and yet with that country feeling."

"The children like it here too, but they will leave soon," she said. "We may lose Jim sooner than you think."

Thank goodness, I was blessed with an adventurous spouse. The moment the question of building and retirement came up, her face lit up, "When do we start looking for a lot?" The thought of building again threw us both into a new spirit of comradeship. Learning again the art of meaningful conversation, we enjoyed this change which is often neglected or missing even in a good a marriage. We sat at the kitchen counter and wrote down four questions: when, where, and how?

"The *where* should be easy for us to decide." Anne said. "We both enjoy country living, and having more land would keep us occupied with our garden, or as you say, orchard."

"As for hobbies," I said. "country sounds even better, since my telescope worked better away from city lights. Retirement is a time to do the projects you enjoy and explore the deeper meaning of life,"

"Most of this evades us when we work for a living." Anne said. "You spoke about lower home assessments. Does this mean in the country, we can build a larger retirement home?"

Since we always valued space in our living area, we saw more clearly that city living was not for us. Several trips to Big Bear mountain taught us, and the children about nature, we'll not forget. We all enjoyed nature and wildlife while camping, but being further away from cultural centers would hurt at times.

"Oh yes," Anne injected. "I remember our camping trips and the sight of a red-tailed hawk soaring in the sky? I say, that's a good tradeoff for the loss of some social events."

The size of our future dwelling was tougher to determine. We enjoyed a spacious home, and the lower cost of land, would favor the size factor. We didn't want to downgrade our lifestyles too much when we retired. And the prices of country lots must be lower than we see in the city. With the economy of today, imagine the prices of acreage ten years from now?

Funding is more complicated. Middle-income Americans always look for ways to save money. We worked and saved carefully during our productive years, with an eye to the time when we could look back with pride on our achievements, reassured that our nest-egg would take care of us. Like most people our age, we didn't want to disturb our investments at this time of life.

Sure, it will be a tough decision to sell some of our income property. As I write, I'm surprised at our impulsiveness. Without second thoughts or regrets, years before I retire, we pushed on with plans to buy land, and start building our home, as a weekend retreat.

Loan Application After Age Fifty

We have many options in financing the construction of a retirement home. The best and least troublesome, is to borrow on your existing home. Since most banks will not loan to owners, lacking a licensed general contractor. Selling the 'Old Homestead' is one way, or a home equity loan, another. At times that mutual fund that's not doing too well might be ready to sell

An owner-builder may be able to convince a local bank to loan money for construction. We had used this approach when building our first home. By proving to the bank that we had completely framed our home, using our money, we received a construction loan.

Building supplies were paid through the voucher system. This worked fine, though several times the suppliers said they had to wait for their money. We found later that the lender was slow to inspect our progress at the building site. However, eventually, everyone got paid, and we finished our beautiful home.

There is another plus in getting a bank construction loan; interest is paid only on money you used. Example, you used $2,400 for forms and concrete the first month. By the time the billing reached the bank, usually the second month, interest for that month at say 11 percent would be only $22. It is better than an equity loan of say $70,000 on your present home. Immediately you owe the first month's interest for that amount. At 11 percent that would be $642. Looking at it with a frugal eye, you have saved $620, using the bank's money.

Another advantage using bank's money, you pay interest only on the balance, with no principal payments. Too, a construction-loan interest it part of the building cost, so you can use the loan money to pay the interest.

When we applied for a construction loan on our first home, framing had already been completed. Knowing we were doing our own building, our bank allowed nine months for completion. My full-time job made it tough to meet that kind of deadline. I took a three-week vacation that summer. Working every day with a little help from the family, we finished the home on time. We were told later that a couple of weeks delay would not have been a problem with that bank.

Be Your Own Banker

An owner-builder can get a lot of information on financing from mortgage brokers; even small local banks are often friendly to an established patron. The easiest however, is to have your own assets you may have amassed during those productive years.

A couple we know wanted to refinance their home to buy a new car and take a European trip. Their bank offered home-equity loans with no points or appraisal fees. Having banked there for many years, they visited the loan officer. It had been some time since their last home loan, and the thick folder of application forms bowled them over.

"You won't believe the list of forms the bank gave me to complete." Said my friend. Many documents were in duplicate and triplicate. Like, request for verification of Employment 3) Request for Verification of Deposit 4) Checking and Saving Account Information 5) Credit Authorization Form 6) Real Estate Property Owned 7) Real Estate Loan Rating 8) Real Estate Appraisal Request Authorization 9) Legal Vesting. (Title information) 10) Securities Certification 11) Notification of Closest Relative 12) Impound Account Agreement 13) Housing Financial Discrimination Act Of 1977

Voluntary Information for Government Monitoring The loan officer also gave them three helpful booklets: Settlement Cost Information, Adjustable Rate Mortgage, and Residential Loan Requirements Information.

Looking at the above, Bank loans of today, are another good reason to use your own money if you can. Saving before retirement, and preparing for that wonderful day of freedom from financial worries is a grand idea. We build our second home as the money came in. Why not buy a truckload of concrete blocks, and when the supply ran out, buy another.

On a new high, nothing was going to deter us. My cautious wife and I took turns backsliding several times. Our bold move in our middle years did shakes me up a little, especially knowing I still had to wait several years before retiring. Yes, I was a fireball when it came to building a home, but will I have the energy to build after working hours?

"But honey, we could start planning our home before we retire." I argued. "This way we could have a weekend retreat, a place in the country everyone talks about."

"A good point," Anne said. "That way we can also get used to the new area before retirement. The way some of these outlying communities were expanding, acreage prices would be prohibitive a couple of years from now."

The idea of a weekend retreat became more intriguing every time we spoke of it, injecting enthusiasm in our daily lives. Dinner talk consisted of designing ideas for the kitchen pantry.

"You know how much I enjoy my dressing room with a vanity," My better-half injected. "And this time, please don't forget my kitchen pantry."

Though we hadn't begun to build, our lives took on new meaning. We couldn't wait to come home from work to exchange ideas, or think up new building sites to visit. To see my drawing board in the observatory, my hands itched to draw plans for our retirement home.

As I sat down to draw, I got a surprised look from my spouse, who knew well that this would begin a new chapter in our lives. I too down to draw, had this strange sensation that I had been here before. It had been more than ten years since I designed our present home. And, what about this observatory and retreat-room, will we plan for another? I've spent many hours here searching the night sky, or painting portraits of our children. A pang of guilt nudged me momentarily as I carefully tacked down the paper to the drawing board. This home had served us well, and like an old friend, we will hardly relish the idea to move to our new one.

In the beginning of the 20th century, many schools of architecture preached rigorous originality, inspiring some students to new heights of creativity. To succeed, they were told, a new approach to structural design and individual thinking was needed. Yet, fearing ridicule, this was seldom practiced by many architects.

The skyscraper with its cubism and so-called purism had become popular at this time. The design of the private home however, became the focal point of architects. The most prominent: Henry Richardson, Louis Sullivan, and Frank Lloyd Wright. Because of their unorthodox methods of blending the home structure into natural surroundings, acceptance by contemporaries was sadly lacking. Perhaps some thought that having to compete with nature would take away from the home's original concept.

Wright was by far the most notable maverick of that time. Some of the more conventional builders shied away from his new approach. The gingerbread, Victorian and Neo-Classic home styles were still favored by most. Surprisingly, this Romantic-Classic trend continued through the thirties, and forties, giving notoriety to those defecting to new creative thinking.

Several books are available on Wright's contribution to design. I enjoyed one enough to read a second time with the same relish. His Fallingwater at Bear Run, Pennsylvania, made a historical statement in residential design. Its placement was close to complete harmony with nature. How did a man in that era of conformity possess such creative sensitivity? His genius will no doubt inspire future generations in his profession.

Then again, nobody is perfect. While studying Wright's photos of the Guggenheim Museum, I asked myself what he may have had in mind when he designed such a waste of space. I felt he carried his license of creativity a bit too far! If designed differently, it could have housed double the amount of art. Did the New York city fathers think this man was infallible?

As society advances, more and more emphasis is on the design and quality of the home. One's home and its environment is no doubt a statement of one's peace of mind. Many of us wonder why dwellers of inferior housing have problems lifting themselves from such surroundings. Is it a loss of hope? Or a mindset influenced by the inferior dwellings they occupy?

Winifred Gallager's book, *The power of Place* Poseidon Press, examines the psychological impact of city vs. rural living. She also touches on how climate, change of seasons, and space effect the human psyche. Whether one is growing up, or has already matured, adequate, and well lighted living space would add to their quality of life.

How can we elevate our thinking, and develop philosophies in a room with five others, while wondering where our next meal will come from? To those who improve their social status with education, and a move to new neighborhood, I say thank God. He gave them that unique quality and character to break away from that mindset, and the ability to visualize new surroundings for their bodies and spiritual awareness.

In the Third World, the poor usually build their homes with the help of relatives or neighbors, often using the barter system and salvaged materials. For them, there is seldom a mortgage, or an interest rate to worry about. Yet many must share their meager dwelling with relatives on order to survive.

In our age of specialization, we're lumped into cubby holes where we perform our menial tasks. I say with that kind of background, it's a miracle any of us become Vise Presidents of a corporation which had imprisoned us. Mortgages cost one third of our income, usually show our income bracket, and lumps us into groups . . . Many of us reach a point in our financial struggle, one h we see as hopeless, where the desire for a better home loses its importance. The price is too high when we must sacrifice our wellbeing to pay high mortgage payments.

Today's economics has fragmented our society to a point of no return. Husband and wife must work, often leaving the children to fend for themselves. Financial and career pressures put us on edge, creating a sinful divorce rate.

It was not always like this. Would you believe, I remember the 40s and 50s when most mothers stayed at home until the last child was in school. The husband return from work with a tense look, often greeted his wife's open arms, soothing his ruffled ego, brought on a hectic workday.

Today's working couple endures a different lifestyle. A rough workday plus a drive in a maddening traffic, can put anyone on edge. One wrong word from either and tempers fly, making retractions of such words impossible. The children are the ones who suffer in a family breakup.

Statistics from FBI show the crime rate for the young has zoomed while that over age 30 remained the same. Is the high cost of housing, and parents working causing this increase? There is no firm evidence of this; but most are sure the direction our society is heading may be partly caused by both parents working.

Though the ready-built home trend remains strong, some Americans still choose to build their own. It takes a persistent kind of person to tackle such a time-consuming project, but all that is needed are people wanting to fulfill their dreams of a better life/ With desire and drive most of us can build a spacious and well lighted dwelling even in today's burdensome economy.

Different Strokes for . . .

In California, a 2,000-square-foot home may cost up to $400,000 depending on the proximity to the coast. As productive members of society, we must pay these prices and commute many miles to work. When we plan for retirement, we should search for less developed areas. Many can no longer afford 35 to 40 percent of our income for housing and taxes.

For some, a mobile home park, or a condominium may be a desirable place to retire. A bonus for those who enjoy frequent travel, most such places provide security while away and recreation facilities while at home.

To be near their children, some retirees sell their homes to buy, or rent in mobile home park, This may not have been their original plan, I don't think retirees have to lower their expectations because they want to be near their children.

Many California young people are leaving for Oregon and Washington to search for jobs, and avoid high-priced housing and traffic. I urge our fifty plus people to be flexible in their approach to retirement, and study all aspects of various options. Express your ideas freely with your partner to see if they mesh with what you believe retirement should be. Personality traits are as varied as are the stars in heaven. If you enjoy travel six months out of the year, buy a condominium and relish the life of leisure. If you and your spouse enjoy the outdoors, love gardening, decorating, and creative hobbies, I suggest you build that dream retirement home in the less expensive outskirts.

If both husband and wife have made up their minds on location, style of home, and its cost. I wish to reiterate the mistake some make; they usually don't go far enough with their plans. We have friends that were too cautious in their planning, became unhappy with their little place, resold and moved into a more desirable home. Do not short change yourself with a restrictive lifestyle. With early financial planning, and wise use of resources, you can make retirement an adventure you've dreamed of.

The Right Size

As owner-builders proceed with different stages of planning, they may go overboard on the size of a home. Call it irrational rationalization, or building mania, but this happened to us twice in our lifetime. Still, we never regretted our building decisions. We felt that people often do not go far enough for their own good, or think too small while trying to save money. However, the final result is not quite what they really wanted.

A decision to actually build that retirement home forces us to make some far-reaching moves. Dipping into savings for the building lot could be threatening to some, as could be converting a mutual fund into cash. The most mind-rattling is selling your present home, and rent one near the building site. All these options might rock that proverbial boat we often enjoy in the middle years. What we did, we sold our home and bought a duplex closer to our building site.

The cost of the building site? How much money will we need for construction? What is the source of our building fund? How will I and my spouse cope with the stress of building? Which phases of building will we contract out? How will we manage our time between our jobs, our family, and the building site? Will we design our home, or hire a professional? How much of the construction will we actually do?

This is a good time to sit down with your spouse to exchange ideas, and express desires that may not be known till now. Many couples need such a verbal intercourse to mend some of the emotional bridges that may have been damaged in the past with thoughtless remarks, or deeds. We might see a joint venture of building in our middle years, a blessing in disguise.

As we have already built two homes, we wish to pass on to you some of the mounting excitement, and t intimate closeness we experienced while planning our building projects.

Unless you're already on the verge of breakup, those of you who wish to take that first bold step may find a welcome renewal of your marital relationship. You could be thoroughly surprised to welcome each day as it unfolds with new challenges. And like us, you'll see your partner with new eyes, and reach a new plateau in your relationship.

You may enter some vigorous debates with your spouse in the planning stage, about the style or location of your dwelling. However, I wouldn't fret about this. Your marriage had already been tested by time, and should endure. When you finish, and move into your new home, your building experience, and pride in your custom home will last through life, making this your last major effort to significantly add to your happiness.

CHAPTER FOUR

MATERIAL CHOICES

In the past, the choice of building material was usually dictated by what was available near the building site. If it was in the forest, the builders would use wood; if the terrain was rocky, stone was chosen.

Today's efficient transportation allows the modern builder to use exotic materials at reasonable cost, from across the country or the seas. A homeowner in Long Island can easily order redwood from the Pacific Northwest. We have bought lumber stamped in the Philippines, Malaysia and Africa. Our ceramic tile, marble, and cement come from Asia, Europe and Latin America.

The most common material used in our country is wood, masonry, and concrete. With the exception of wood, few of these can be used as a sole building substance.

Adobe. High desert more or less described our future location, allowing us several choices of building materials. Two of our neighbors, used adobe bricks from a manufacturer in the valley below. The only lumber used was for the roof structure, doors and cabinets, thus saving many trees from the lumberman's axe. These homes were uniquely different, adding an interesting variety to our community. Few building materials however, can be called perfect.

"We lost many square feet in living area with our thick 16-inch adobe walls." remarked Dean Harriman. Another drawback: the county assessor measures the living area from the outside to outside walls. Our neighbors pay property taxes on square footage they cannot use.

If hot weather persists for many days, the walls would finally get hot and remain so during the night. This however, is not common on our mountain; summer nights can vary by as much as 40 degrees from day temperatures. After eleven enjoyable years in an adobe home, our friends show their "Adobe haciendas." with pride.

Tamped Earth. Imagine using the soil from the site to build your home. The possibilities are mind-boggling. This was our other building option, and we had enough of the right kind of soil on our large lot to build it. We never really researched this method. An article I read showed that so many parts of sand and clay type soil are thoroughly mixed, made slightly damp. The mixture is then shoveled into formed walls, and tamped in four-to-five-inch layers until firm. To retain smooth vertical walls, 3/4-inch, 4-by-8-foot plywood forms are braced vertically 16 inches on center with 2-by-4 lumber, held together by metal ties.

After exterior walls and partitions are tamped to the correct height, the plywood forms are removed, and used as sheathing for the roof structure. Roof eaves with larger than normal overhang protect the exterior earth walls from the weather.

Books on tamped-earth construction can be found in many libraries. Before any serious plans are made, see your local building department for codes and special permit information.

Stick Lumber. A well insulated wood-frame home can be as comfortable in cool New England states as in the semitropical sunbelt. Probably the most popular method in America is using wood, making the precut 92 1/2 inch stud the most popular in the building industry A carpenter will need nine of these studs, as they are called, and three 12-foot 2 by 4s, one for the bottom plate and two top plates, to put up a 12-foot-long wall. These are easily nailed together on the floor then tilted up to form the wall. Thus, much less lumber is used in frame-type construction than in a log house.

Post and Beam. This is another option when using wood. I have always admired this method as the design allows large open areas without supporting posts to take up living space. This method puts the heaviest loads over posts rather than on the bearing walls, creating large window areas to the outside.

There may be a costly drawback to the post & beam method: if beam span exceeds 24 or more feet, a spec sheet from a structural engineer is required. Most plan-checkers in the building and safety bureau will insist on several types of metal bracing and bolts to tie the beams together. In an open-beam ceiling, a ¼ inch by 1 ½ inches wide, by 24 inch metal straps are acceptable to secure together the rafters.

Log. Some of us would like to return to frontier days and build the traditional log house. We can order precut, and erect it in a couple of weeks. There are several advantages to logs. The cellular structure of wood, eight inches thick gives good insulation year around. In case of fire, it takes a long time for that size log to burn, giving the owner time to put it out and save the home.

Stone. My wife and I always admired stone homes. They have that natural look and feel of belonging to the setting, especially when treated with a complementary exterior design. My immediate response, is the blessed permanence, plus security this type home radiates for the dweller.

To build an entire home of stone would be costly, needing double walls for insulation and steel reinforcement. One could use inexpensive masonry inner walls, then one or two-inch Styrofoam insulation panels between the outside stone veneers. If your building lot, has a plentiful supply of stone, go for it. This type of structure will use about 75 percent less lumber and spare many trees.

Why Use concrete blocks?

An incident in our lives was the reason we choose to build with concrete blocks, reinforced with steel. Some years ago a fire destroyed a large building in the town below. The night sky glowed and flames leaped 50 feet into the smoky sky, making this a frightening scene from our home. Not much would remain of that structure, we thought. The next morning, when we checked the damage, we couldn't believe our eyes. The lumber yard's exterior walls were standing tall, while the roof structure was completely gone. With all the dry lumber and paint, the heat must have been tremendous, yet the concrete block walls looked solid. The owners applied for permits to rebuild the roof, and soon the building was restored to its original specifications, and the lumber yard was ready business.

My wife and I agreed that if we should ever build again, it would be with be with concrete blocks. Another reason for choosing blocks, could have been my European background, where most homes are of brick and mortar, some several hundred years old.

However, there are problems with masonry walls. Thermal factor: Heat and cold retention, much more than with wood. If the day is hot, so will be the night. Concrete retains heat for a long time. In the cold season, it is more difficult to heat a masonry home unless it is designed for that area, using modern building methods.

Weight. This must be seriously considered if the soil conditions are unstable at the building site. The footings will have to be deeper, and into solid natural grade, reinforced with steel rods.

Using concrete blocks will also increase the cubic yards of concrete needed to support the heavier walls. We must also consider the extra cost of reinforcing steel. If we build with concrete, the use of steel could be more critical should the property be near an earthquake fault. Deformed steel bars are usually competitively priced, but it would be prudent to shop around for bids.

Since 1978, residential builders must provide an inner stud wall or a double masonry wall, spaced few inches apart for insulation. This will add significantly to the cost, but the space between will make electrical wiring and plumbing much easier.

If local building codes permit, a builder can laminate a one-inch Styrofoam insulation on the outside walls, then wrap with paper and wire mesh, so the walls could take stucco, (author's untested idea.) One drawback with stucco walls, they are not recommended in frost zones, as they are nearly impossible to seal against moisture. Once this seeps in, the wire mesh used as wrap will deteriorate, and severe freeze will expand and disintegrate the stucco.

I called Orco Block, (my old supplier) to ask if they sold the new type of concrete blocks with the Styrofoam. They did, but naturally, the cost is higher, Still, a builder could save a lot of time and money with this, as only a single wall is legally required. But building with masonry do have a bonus: a) Concrete blocks are fireproof and one of the most durable building materials on earth. b) Almost anyone can lay the blocks, and at their own pace. c) Concrete does not warp in the sun, and rain does not expand it. d) We save the American forests with its use. e) The last and most important: time is not a factor for the couple planning their retirement home. Ordering a few concrete blocks every month, they'd not need a construction loan, or touch their precious assets. With good financial planning, one can/build as the money comes in. Imagine completely building your retirement home with a monthly building budget. All the funds you receive from the sale of your present residence can be put into a trust fund when you retire. There is no need to tap into it for building, and the interest money it provides can make life much more enjoyable. Too good to be true? We know of people that built their home this way. Their lot was not fully paid when the home was finished; that money was used for building materials. It would be advisable to check with the building department about permit extensions. There may be a small charge to keep your building permit on the books.

The argument for a concrete or masonry home certainly has merit. Many countries in Europe are proud to show excellent masonry structures built in the ninth and tenth centuries. In Rome we were somewhat astonished to find the Pantheon, built in 27 BC, in perfect condition. The dome, with its 60-foot roof aperture, the only window. What is the roof structure made of? If you guess concrete, you are right.

Many think that Portland cement named after an English city, was actually discovered in England. Yet, Roman builders used concrete many centuries before them. They ground sea shells into fine powder, mixed this with washed sand and gravel, and produced a durable concrete, one lasting thousands of years.

Our guide told us that the Pantheon is the most perfectly preserved building in Rome. You could ask, Why would we want our home to last, 2,000 years, when we can save a lot of time and hard work building a wood-frame home. My answer; "Generations after your passing, the home you and your spouse designed and built using concrete and steel will still be there. It will carry your own spiritual signature like an artistic statement for a millennium or more. Then there is that marvelous thought as you imagine the beautiful growth of Douglas Fir still standing, all because you built from the most plentiful material on earth. I believe God, along with your descendants will bless you for your insight

HOUSE PLANS, SITE CHOICES, AND SUB CONTRACTING

ariations in floor plans and exterior design can be mind-boggling to a potential builder. Still, some may want to design their own, expressing their unique ideas of what a home should be.

However, one has many ways to acquire house plans. In Chapter Five, I provide five plans free to copy. If you once took high school drafting, you have my permission to redraw them. All you need is to check for building codes in your area, get a sample copy of any building plans, and you are ready to draw.

Plans drawn by an architect can go as high as 10% of the cost of your home, A draftsman will charge up to a $1000 for 4 copies. With a little research, you and your spouse can design your dream home, and take the credit.

Another way to get plans, try the many publishing houses. Some catalogs may be free, or for a small fee refunded upon purchase. I've seen prices for plans from $60 to $95 for the first set, and about $30 for additional copies. Seldom will such plans be accepted by all area building departments, and may need modification to meet local building codes.

A builder should have at least four sets when applying for a construction permit. I think for some builders, it may be best to buy a cheap readymade plans for their conceptual value. By closely studying them, you can learn from them, or if you wish, you can try and design your dream home. This is what we did before building out two homes. In our second however, our friends said we went overboard, and we agree: A 3000

Sq. Foot Mediterranean mini-villa, resembling a Geek temple, is hardly what one would call, an ordinary home. (see the last chapter)

My thought however, as owner-builder designing his home, drawing my home plans can turn into a delightful home-building experience. Especially if one is married, and seeks input from his spouse.

"I love my kitchen, "Anne remarked. "But you forgot my pantry"

"Pantry?"

"Honey, living on a mountaintop, we'll need much room for cereal boxes, and canned foods."

My wife and I had more discussions about floor plans, like, "I love the classic columns in the front. But why are you putting the two in the entry way?"

Sure I had a hard time finding a magazine showing classic columns in the entry. After buying one covering classic mansions, I won my case.

Many of us have found pleasure drawing sketches when decorating, or remodeling our homes. In building your own, you can test your skills in designing your dream home. An AARP study shows that many future retirees preferred to stay in their present home. Yet, a quick look at the average home design tells us that for some, this would be highly unlikely. What was once a delightful floor plan to navigate, as we grow older, becomes an exercise in futility?

Many older homes are multi-storied, or split-level structures, with too many doors and walls, which become obstacles for the elderly. Doors can be removed easily but to remove walls require structural understanding as walls most support ceiling and roof.

To make architectural changes would be costly for most, since income has dwindled to bare essentials. This hit home when my mother needed a chairlift after her last illness. She loved her home and did not want to move. A bathroom downstairs would also be helpful but again too costly.

Many of us see ourselves as once nimble, may occasionally trip on plush rugs causing us to feel foolish, or worse, cause an injury. Clearly it would be advantageous to install tightly woven carpets and dispose of all throw-rugs. As eyesight and alertness dwindles, it would be wise to remove dim light bulbs, opaque venetian blinds. In my volunteer work, I see many elderly live in homes with small windows, restricting daylight.

"Why is it so dark here?" I asked an elderly woman, while a volunteer for meals On Wheels.

"I wanted a more modern apartment," She replied. "This is what I can afford."

Top. With a view to Catalina Island, framing was a joy.
Bottom. Imagine our happiness, moving in from our tiny guesthoue

The happy day we surveyed our
acres on a California mountaintop

After the concrete slab is poured, a new house-framer begins

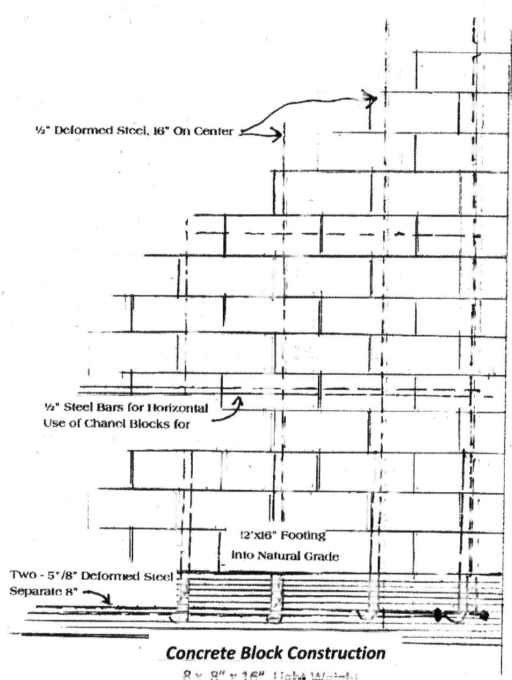

½" Deformed Steel, 16" On Center

½" Steel Bars for Horizontal
Use of Chanel Blocks for

!2'x!6" Footing
Into Natural Grade

Two - 5"/8" Deformed Steel
Separate 8"

Concrete Block Construction

2 x 8" x 16" Light Weight
Channel type for Steel rods,
Plumbing, and Electrical Conduits

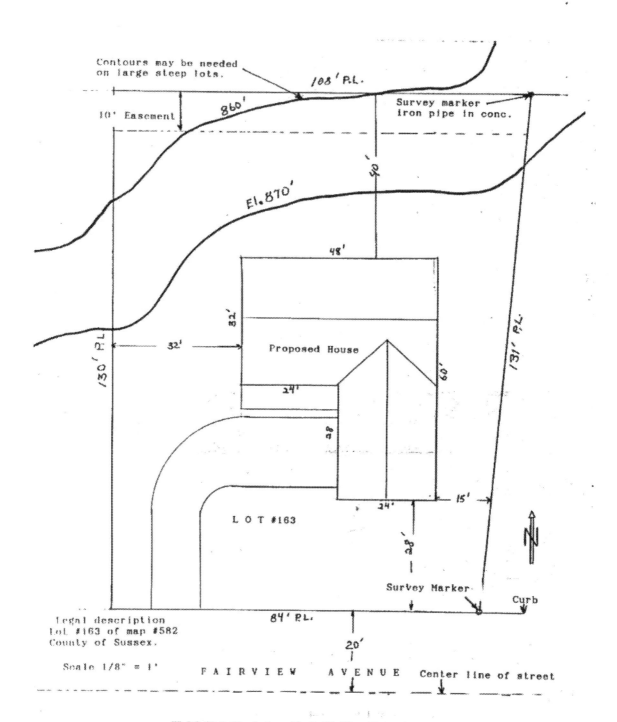

TYPICAL PLOT PLAN

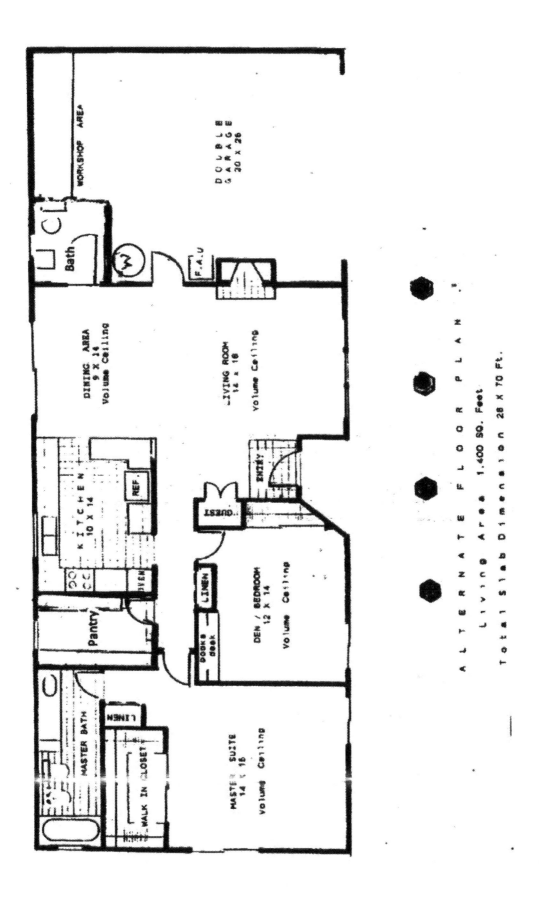

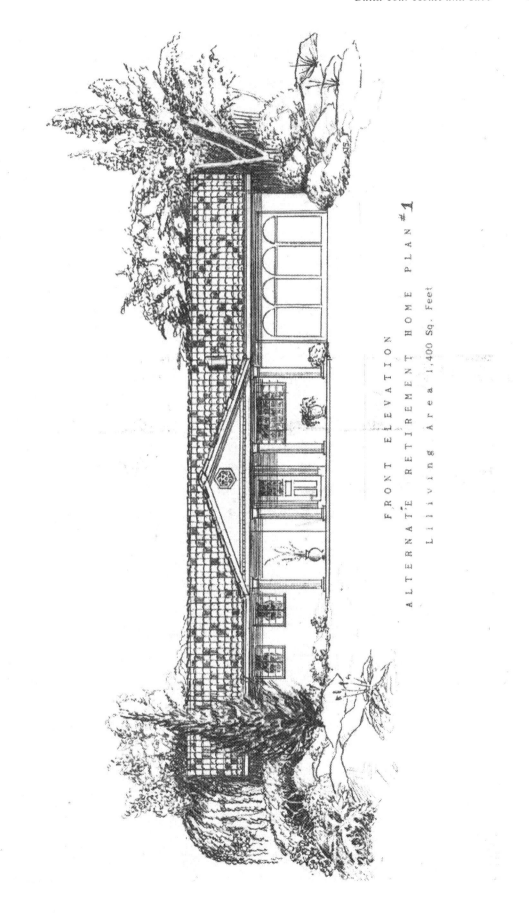

FRONT ELEVATION
ALTERNATE RETIREMENT HOME PLAN #1
Living Area 1,400 Sq. Feet

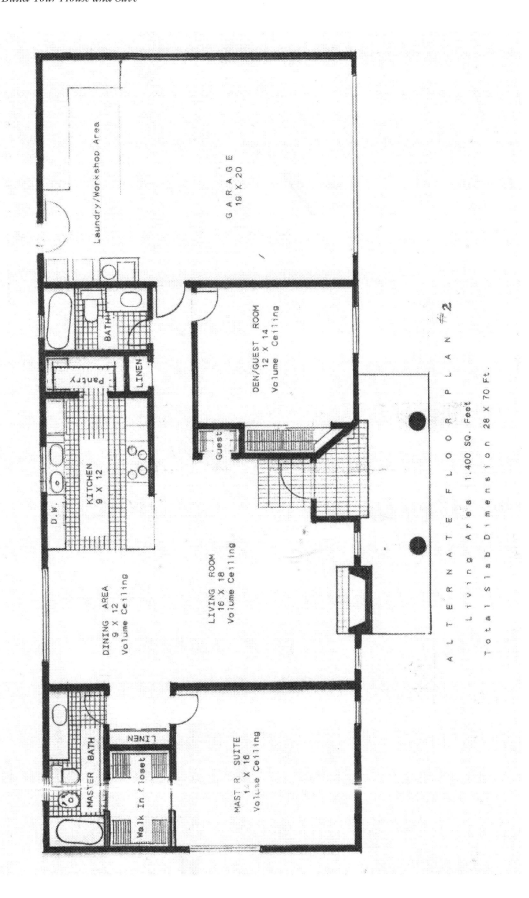

ALTERNATE FLOOR PLAN #2
Living Area 1,400 SQ. Feet
Total Slab Dimension 28 X 70 Ft.

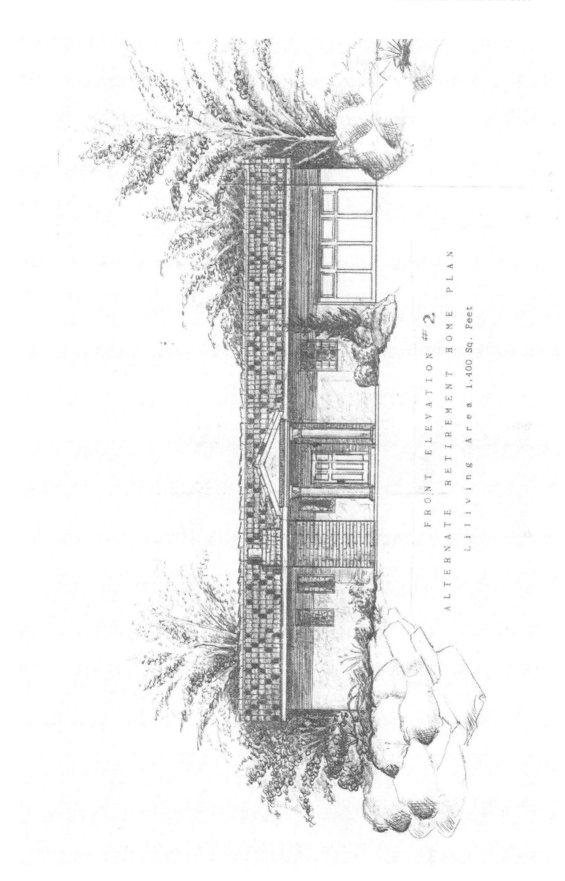

FRONT ELEVATION #2
ALTERNATE RETIREMENT HOME PLAN
Living Area 1,400 Sq. Feet

ALTERNATE FLOOR PLAN # 3
Owner's Liv. Area 1,208 Sq.Ft - Separate Suite Area 364 Sq.Ft
Total Liv. Area 1,572 Sq.Ft - Slab Area 2,080 Sq.Ft

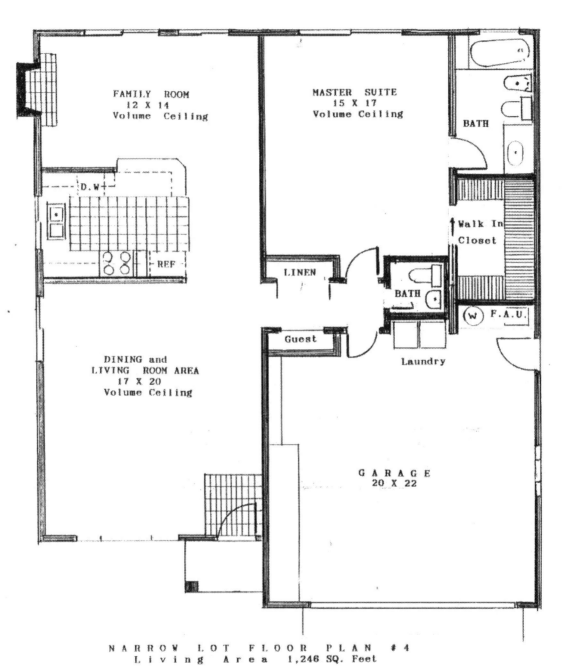

FAMILY ROOM
12 X 14
Volume Ceiling

MASTER SUITE
15 X 17
Volume Ceiling

BATH

D.W

REF

Walk In
Closet

LINEN

BATH

DINING and
LIVING ROOM AREA
17 X 20
Volume Ceiling

Guest

Laundry

W   F.A.U.

G A R A G E
20 X 22

N A R R O W   L O T   F L O O R   P L A N   # 4
L i v i n g   A r e a   1,246 SQ. Feet

A SPACIOUS ONE BEDROOM WITH ONE AND A HALF BATHS

NARROW LOT FLOOR PLAN #4
Living Area 1,246 SQ. Feet

A SPACIOUS ONE BEDROOM WITH ONE AND A HALF BATHS

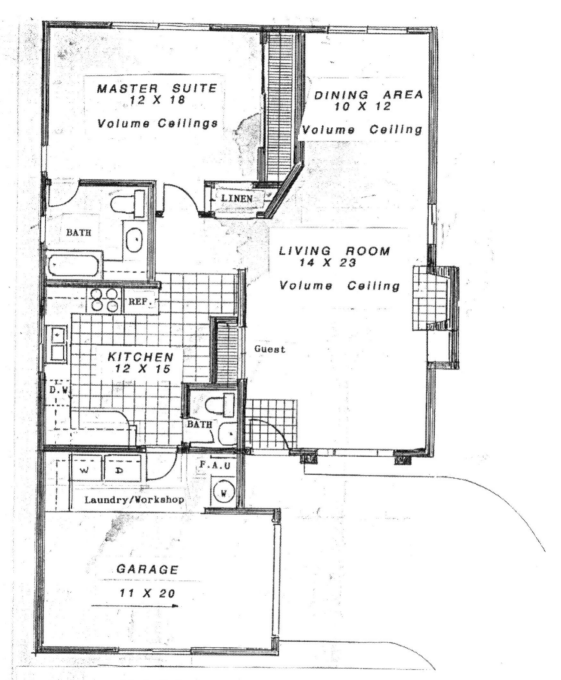

N A R R O W   L O T   P L A N #5
Living Area 1,008 Sq. Ft.
A Spacious Master Suite And Large Kitchen

MODERN COLONIAL 1,800 Sq. Feet
3 & 4 Living Styles

First owner-built La Habra Heights

The author framed this 2,720 Sq. Ft, in a litte more than a month, after work, and on weekends. His happy wife eagerly helped him tilt up the walls, and later nail the roof shingles.

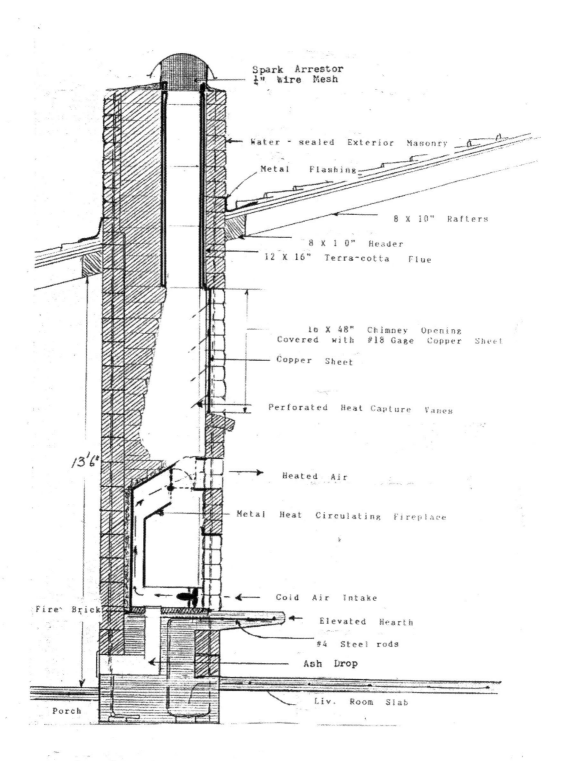

Spark Arrestor
¼" Wire Mesh

Water - sealed Exterior Masonry

Metal Flashing

8 X 10" Rafters

8 X 1 0" Header
12 X 16" Terra-cotta Flue

16 X 48" Chimney Opening
Covered with #18 Gage Copper Sheet

Copper Sheet

Perforated Heat Capture Vanes

Heated Air

Metal Heat Circulating Fireplace

Cold Air Intake

Elevated Hearth

#4 Steel rods

Ash Drop

Liv. Room Slab

13'6"

Fire Brick

Porch

CROSS-SECTION OF SPECIAL FIREPLACE

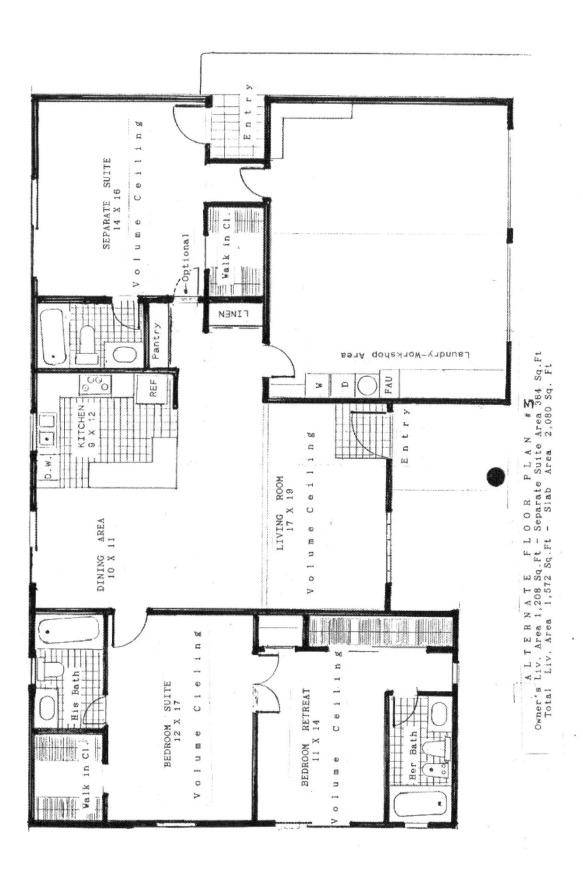

ALTERNATE FLOOR PLAN #3
Owner's Liv. Area 1,208 Sq.Ft — Separate Suite Area 364 Sq.Ft
Total Liv. Area 1,572 Sq.Ft — Slab Area 2,080 Sq.Ft

NARROW LOT FLOOR PLAN # 5
Living Area 1,008 SQ. Feet

After we installed lever-type doorknobs in our first home, I can't imagine why anyone would want round knobs. We can now open doors with both hands full by pushing on the lever with a package or an elbow.

The past few years, home design trends have now evolved to a more open feeling, giving future retirees options to suit their needs. As our lifestyles change, retirement home plans must be approached differently, Some may enjoy excellent health while others handicapped by an illness, will seriously consider a floor plan that will ease their condition.

Our experience in designing and drawing plans for our retirement home, may help others decide whether to do their own preliminary. and final drawing, or order them from an architect.

Many office-supply stores have graph paper that simplifies the drawing of preliminary floor plans. I chose 1/4th inch squares on a 16-by-20-inch graph paper, making each square equal one square foot, sufficient for a medium-sized home.

For a drafting board, I used a 30 by 40-inch piece of smooth plywood, padded with several sheets of paper. A three-foot T-square is sufficient for most drawing. Find a sturdy table with a comfortable chair, in a quiet room. With pencils and sharpener at hand, a compass, and a soft eraser for all those errors and mind changes, you'll be ready for designing your dream home.

For ideas of tried-and-true floor plans, I would study home magazines or do-it-yourself periodicals. You may have admired a friend's home with a striking floor plan, and can use the best features of several. One can say that no idea is totally original, but it is still illegal to copy an architect's, or draftsperson's plan in its totality without permission. Whereas my floor plans are free to use. Choose one you like, and improve on it.

I have not seen readymade plans specifically designed for retirement homes. In this chapter are six conceptual designs that are free to copy and refine by the reader. Consult with your spouse on the style of home you want, and make sure the floor plan is agreeable to both. It is vital to go over the plans, and discuss all the details thoroughly. Once the building department plan checker approves the specifications, changes will be harder to make.

Decide how to orient the house on your lot. If your street runs east and west, a front-facing south is to your advantage. This may place your bedroom on the north, with a cooler evening in your favor. Some floor plans show the master bedroom in the front, so if your home faces north, the reverse is true. Many floor plans have bedrooms in the rear of the house, usually with large sliding glass doors to patio, and back yard. If you own a lot on which the front would face north, design the floor plan so your bedrooms face north and the front street.

This works much the same way if your street runs north to south. The front of your home will face east or west depending on what side of the street you are on. In colder climates, this could be reversed. In winter it is ideal to have bedrooms face south, as the low winter sun can warm them to save fuel. However, with double or triple pane windows, along with the use of insulation, orientation of your home is not that important. If you lot has a view, you can forgo all the above and take advantage of a beautiful view.

"I like our present location of our bedroom." Anne said, looking at the floor plan. "We wake up each day with that cheerful sunrise in our bdroom."

"Yes, with an acre or more we have more freedom to do that." I reassured. "If we face the home to the south, it will put the master suite in the cool northeast."

This location is ideal in hot climates, as north rooms are cooler all day and into the evenings. We also enjoy a sliding glass door to our patio and back yard from the master suite.

The roof style and exterior walls is your next important decision. If cost is a consideration, go for the least expensive roof and siding materials. For exterior siding, the 4-by-8-foot sheet textured plywood is a good choice. Its many surface textures and finishes will save money and installation time. Get several bids from several building, and supply stores to get the best prices. This type siding goes up nearly twice as fast as vertical board-and-batten, even quicker when using the horizontal eight-inch tongue-and-groove board. The rough-cut finish eliminates the need for frequent painting as paint clings longer to rough surfaces.

When specifying roof material, asphalt shingles are the most popular for single dwellings. They are the easiest to apply, and the best grade will still be less expensive than others. Roofing is a competitive business; if you don't want to do the roof yourself, do get several bids before building begins.

The choice of roofing was very important to us since our home was located next to a forest. In dry summer months, we had constant threat of forest fires which spread quickly with mountain breezes.

Many areas require specific codes on roof shingles to meet Class A, B, and C standards of fire resistance. 'A' is the most resistant and costly. If this is a problem, consult local building codes for minimum requirements.

The costlier Class A roof will also have better appearance and durability. The double-layer strips and thicker mineral surfaces, will give the appearance of a more textured roof. All bundled roofing comes with concise instruction for installation, giving the owner a chance to save money.

The Joy of Doing Your Own Plans

I was faced with a vital question. Can I draw the final plans for our weekend retreat, or should we hire an architect, or a draftsperson? This depends much on the individual. The cost of custom-home plans can go over $3,000, depending on the size and location. Many professionals charge 10 percent of the building cost. This alone may persuade you to draw your own.

Those of us who took a drafting class in high school, will probably draw and design our own, especially when we can save several thousand dollars. And too, the challenge to do it yourself s can be rewarding, If you are an innovator and feel creative, try one drawing to see how it looks and feels. Another plus in doing your own plans. An owner-builders will have no problems in understanding their own drawings. If however you are your own contractor, and hire subs to build, have a professional draw from your preliminary sketches. You may still be credited for the original design, but a professional drawing will be more concise to building trades people. There may be minor building code corrections that might have been overlooked; a professional, familiar with local codes will correct the errors, or even design problems.

Drawing plans for our first home taught me several lessons. Be neat and precise, with the best possible detail, and check with the building department for specification sheets in all phases of construction.

When we decided to build our retirement home, I drew several plans considering our lifestyle and uses, and kept it simple. A step saving kitchen is one possible idea, another a larger workshop for the perpetual tinkerer or cabinet maker, or a guest-hobby room for that creative woman of the house. Some find it difficult to read floor plans. I wish to show how easy it really is. Unlike reading a book where you start at the top to read the first sentence, you begin at the bottom and entrance of the structure. Find the page with floor plan Number Three, make certain all the printing is right side up, and put you at the bottom by the entrance. Imagine you are on a high ladder looking down on a home with no ceilings. Let your eyes wander through the front entry and through the living room. You are now in the hall and find all the doors to the different rooms opened. Turn right in the hall and see the linen closet, or right again to the garage.

Back in the hall, you see the pantry door ahead, and on the right, the linen closet and proposed separate suite. The word "optional" points to the opened door. You as carpenter may leave this door in or block it for future use. It is quite easy as you face the living room. To the right is the kitchen. Moving ahead through the living-dining area you find the doorway to the master suite.

Plan Three may have many advantages to the retiree. Although I just pulled it out of the hat, as the saying goes, it was a good hat and the more we studied it the more appealing it was. We almost chose it as the one and only, an easy-to-build rectangle, which frugally uses every square foot. The spacious living-dining area with vaulted ceiling gives the feeling of a large home that some would like, but could not afford in retirement. An optional living room fireplace can replace the linen closet in the retreat room wall. The kitchen is adequate and shows two exits for easy access and a sliding glass window to a patio.

The idea of a bedroom suite with the retreat area also dazzled us. We married people keep our good qualities and seldom improve on our bad ones. To have the bedroom with a retreat solves the problem of one reading and other watching television. The window can be a larger sliding glass or the more costly French doors. This, however, will deplete the room's wall area and make the placement of the bed and other furniture more of a problem.

The retreat room can be used as a study, a hobby, or that rare moment of contemplation alone. It can also serve as a spare sleeping room for a relative.

His and hers bathrooms are our favorites. I had once heard, "The honeymoon is over when you cease taking showers together, or begin to use the same bathroom"

After traveling abroad, the lady of the house will now appreciate a bidet in her own bath. The narrow window between her bath and the wardrobe is for additional light only, and could be opaque or of stained-glass. His and hers wardrobe closets are also appropriate as often one of us is neater than the other.

Separate Suite

The separate suite is one of the better ideas in floor plan #3. Here the retiree-builder can keep it as a guest room, or rent if income dwindles. And Heaven forbid, children may return for trial separations from a troubled marriage, and can enjoy privacy.

For couples who need extra income, and whose total is under the Social Security limit for married couple, the extra suite is an excellent idea as a room rental. I do not imply that this floor plan is the best, but should be considered if money becomes a problem. If rented for $600 a month, the extra income could total $7,200 a year. More than enough to pay your property tax, or put away for a rainy day.

Did we choose this ideal plan? Certainly not! It was too easy, cost effective and too rational for this irrational couple. Our heads were in the clouds, dreaming of a more noble structure on a California mountaintop, where renting a room would be out of the question.

Material Research

We have many materials from which to choose in our high-tech world. Textures and colors with synthetic materials abound, and some could outlast wood by years, yet look superb as a finished product. Some home magazines have information on new building materials, and show various applications.

While browsing in building-supply places, an owner may find a new and useful product. Do not hesitate; there is still time to change. If it enhances the structure and is more durable, then go for it, especially if the product will save building costs. Making such alterations the owner must notify the building department.

We saw a roof installed on an older home over wooden shingle. Actually a light-weight red tiled roof, by *Decrabond.* Driving by, we could have sworn it was a genuine tile roof. Four-foot sections of steel pressed interlocking tile are granular coated for long life and are easy to install. A full square weighs a lot less than cedar shake shingles.

Our past experience proves that knowing about available building product helps when drawing plans. Most manufacturers are happy to provide builders with spec sheets on their new products.

Aluminum columns we saw in several home magazines looked authentic, lightweight and easy to install. I never checked out prices but the advertised specs were appealing, and no doubt more investigation would have been worthwhile.

We however, did ours the old-fashioned way. We designed and carved our own capitals, and pedestals, then cast them in concrete. For the columns, I assembled wood patterns, then made rubber molds from which we cast two-foot concrete sections of hollow columns. We stacked them in place with mortar over imbedded steel rods and filled them with concrete. Now we will never know if in the next 1,000 years the reinforced concrete or aluminum columns would have lasted longer.

To our surprise, we derived much satisfaction in designing and manufacturing our building material. This may have delayed construction by about six months, but this was no problem as time was not a priority; we had many years before retirement. We provided all the capitols and column sections for our classic home, by casting them in concrete in our back yard of our townhouse.

I recall the day a neighbor approached our fence. "Excuse my asking, but are you manufacturing here in a residential zone?"

I gave him a worried look, trying to think of an appropriate response, "Yes, one can say we are, but you see, these products are not for resale; they're for our own use."

Except for the vibrating casting table, we made very little noise in our work. I asked him if he would please be patient a bit longer. The response was neither positive nor negative; we worried, thinking he might call city hall. Later, when they learned the castings would be columns for our home, our kind neighbors gave us their blessings. Many times, honesty and the right answers prove that people are basically good.

I do not wish to demean the professionals in the building industry. Theirs is a seasonal business, and they must charge high prices, to cover their overhead and investment in equipment. What is written here might save the owner some time and money, and possibly upgrade his proposed retirement home. Our journal about phases of construction and method of acquiring building material could also be helpful to some, as can informing the reader of unforeseen problems we experienced building our two homes.

First Plans

My first drawing of home plans some years ago was a bit disappointing. After several months of drawing, I presented them to city building and safety for a plan check. Ten days later, we had a notice to pick them up and make about 15 corrections, explaining in more detail some parts of the drawing. That's right! I hadn't done my homework. The literature and specification sheets were at the building office, but I just did not know about it, or bothered to ask.

We had plans done by a professional, which I used as a guide for our drawing. Though they helped a lot as a format, our new home would be on a hillside and the drawing had to be treated differently.

If you plan to do your own drawing, do visit your local building department. Ask for all the spec sheets available, and sample sketches on footing, framing, and roofing. Your drawing must show details and location of all plumbing fixtures and electrical service and outlets. Though we could afford a draftsman, I wanted this challenge of designing and drawing. This was one of the building phases I enjoyed very much, and knowing this, my wife didn't want to take this pleasure from me.

Plot Plan Needed

The first step in your building plans would be a plot plan of your lot. It must show the location of the new home, the front, side and rear setback distance in feet. You must show all corner stakes and distances between them, and location of easements and alleys that may show in the original recorded lot description.

The following is list needed for a plot plan:

1 North Arrow 2 Show Existing Survey Hubs 3 Legal description 4 Distance between Buildings 5 Distance to the street 6 Distance from street to the center of street. Height & type of fences-wall 8 Identify the type and use of existing structures 9 Existing building location 10 Names & widths of bordering streets. 11 Property dimensions / boundaries 12 Ally location & widths

A legal description must be attached with the plans. Some may not be favorable for the kind of home you want. Sewer connections and underground utilities must be shown in the plot plan drawing. Usually the seller will provide the lot map or the local planning department will give you a copy for a small fee. It is easy to enlarge it to a 24-by 36-inch from the scale information of the original which also shows the North arrow. If the scale shows that 1 inch = 40 feet, you can make yours 1/8 inch = 1 foot; this scale will give you a presentable drawing for the building department.

If your lot is steep, check with the building department. You may have to provide contour lines (topo map) of the lot for the plot drawing. Often these can be had for a fee from city or county planners. If not, the builder must hire a surveyor team to contour the building site. Your topo or plot plan must also show location of septic tank and leach field if sewers are not available in your area.

A steep site may have to show a drawing of the graded Building pad, indicating how much soil has to be moved, and where it will be placed, as well the direction of water runoff. If more dirt is moved than allowed, a grading permit is needed. This will vary for each location. Our county allowed up to 300 cubic yards of dirt to be moved without a grading permit.

For an average level lot, drawing the plot plan is rather easy. If you can draw your house plans you can do your plot plan.

Why Mediterranean?

For our retirement home, we did the plans phase backward. The usual procedure is to buy the building lot first, then draw plans to suit the building site. As we already knew what kind of home we wanted, our scheme was to find the site to fit our drawing. This wasn't easy; we needed a site with its own knoll, like a pedestal for a Greek temple. This all sounds crazy to the reader, but we were determined to go all the way with our Mediterranean mini-villa look.

The more we thought of it, the more determined we became. "Have we gone too far this time?" Anne asked again, "How will our future neighbors feel about our idea?"

"What worries me," I said, "is what if the building department won't approve our style and method of building?"

The answers we were not sure about; the questions we had to ask to plant our feet firmly on the ground. Anything could happen, but with our optimism pushed in high gear, we were not thinking of Murphy's Law.

You and your partner have drawn preliminary plans and made firm decisions on the size, style, and material choices of your new home. If you enjoy drawing, and have the determination to do the final plans, a book on home drafting could be useful as a reference guide.

Be sure to include your plot plan with legal description of property as your first page of your plans. A few tips that may be helpful to you in this enjoyable phase: a) Get a complete sample of house plans drawn by a professional. This will guide you in your own drawing for clarity and detail. b) Use a hard lead pencil at first, then a soft one for a good contrasting print to outline the important parts. c) Show in detail the foundation outline and plumbing locations, distances and dimensions. d) Show detail of floor plan, locations and size of all windows, doors, partitions and porches. e) Roof structure, bracing and metal straps used. Show pitch of roof and covering used. f) Draw front, rear, and two side elevations. g) Show specifications and material list. h) Double check drawing for completeness and clarity compare with a sample professional drawing. i) Make one copy; examine the quality, and if satisfactory, make four more. This list is not complete but it may give an idea that it can be done with precision. I saw an owner submit plans for a room addition on two 8-by-11 sheets of stationery, surprised to see them accepted by the building department. If you plan to do most of the building, I recommend that you be serious about drawing a well detailed plans. If you are not happy with the first try, a second and more exacting and cleaner one can be made. The pleasure of doing it yourself, is worth the effort, not to mention the $500 to $3,000 you may save.

CHAPTER SIX

SELECTING THE SITE

The importance of selecting the site cannot be stressed enough to the potential home builder. You must see the location as much more important than the design of your home. You can always remodel, add on or change the style after its completion. This does not apply to the location once the home is on the lot. We are more or less stuck with the neighborhood and the future development of the area.

As investors in real estate, we would give our broker notes on what kind of property we were looking for. There were several items we considered important:

Price. The property must be fairly priced for the area, and what you can afford. It must have improvements on it so the potential rent income will help with payments, although this may not apply to everyone.

Location. Check out the neighborhood. Look at adjoining properties and homes. How far is the nearest grocery? How near the auto-wreck and trash dump? As a senior, the location of the nearest hospital is important. Visit the local planning department to see if there is a zone change on the agenda. Some sellers dump properties when rezoning is considered, and property values are affected. If possible, visit your future lot after a heavy rain for damage. Recheck for direction of run-off, or big puddles.

Size. The property must have the lot size and desired zoning potential to allow for additional building or expansion if the terrain permits, possibly for investment.

Utilities. All utilities must be in and paid for with no future liens for street and sewer assessments. If not, a downward adjustment in price is in order.

Some of the above items may not apply when looking for a site for retirement. However, more can be added to the list for the real estate broker when buying. He knows the values of adjoining properties and sometimes their history. In all real estate dealings we had in the past, we purchased only one property without the aid of a broker. Dealing directly with the seller did not work for us. More items on this list could be of help in selecting that unique building lot:

Drainage. Choose a sloping lot with good drainage. If a basement is desired, the cost per square foot is relatively cheap compared with that of the rest of the house. We never have enough storage and hobby space.

Sewers. If the area lacks sewers, the builder must have an acre or more land for a leach field. Check soil for ability to absorb water.

Grading Cost. Check potential building sites for existing views. These lots are more valuable, but may have added grading costs. Once you own view property, you will be hard to please in future acquisitions. Even when looking for investment properties, you may turn down good buys when the location is low and on a dead-end street. Yet this type of house may be very desirable to some young buyers who may desire safety for their children.

Landscaping. Trees are an asset, yet this may add extra cost to move them from a strategic spot of the lot. The initial cost of a wooded lot may be higher in some areas, but having trees near the site provides instant landscaping and will bring natural harmony between the land and your new home.

Water. If the city does not provide water, the buyer should make this a contingency in writing the sales agreement. Should the property have a potential for a working well, a larger lot is needed.

Most regulations say, that a well must be at a certain distance from the septic tank and leach field. Check local ordinance. *Don't Rush.* With a small down payment, and contingencies in the sales agreement, a seller should allow you time to check out those items. It could take several weeks; you should not feel rushed. Nothing can be as wrong as a land purchase gone sour. This is the site of your future retirement home. Make the buying a joyous experience for you and your spouse.

Our Choice

The increasing building activity and traffic in our area were finally getting to us. We wanted at least one-acre minimum for our building lot. Since the cost of this would be prohibitive in coastal cities, we headed for the inland hills, away from the expensive beach towns of Los Angeles County and its bedroom communities.

We drove many miles, and spent endless weekends searching for that dream building site. One beautiful Sunday we went east from the coastal town of San Juan Capistrano, on a picturesque winding road, up into the National Forest.

At the summit, we spotted a real-estate sign that promoted building sites. "Look building lots in the country." Anne pointed joyously. We pulled up closer to read more, and decided to turn right onto a well-graded forestry road. After a short distance this became a dirt road.

"If it's like this the rest of the way," I said. "let's forget it, I don't care for dirt roads," "But, we drove this far, why not see the lots?"

As we drove on, I thought, what's wrong with me? Have I lost my spirit of adventure?

The beautiful drive had a gentle climb to a distant peak. On our left, we could see a lake reflecting a stark blue cloudless sky. Beyond that, an endless view of Riverside and San Bernardino counties, a vast expanse of gently rolling hills with farmed green valleys. Nestled among them were small towns, lakes and more towns. In the distance, shimmering in a light haze, were the cities of Riverside and San Bernardino, against the backdrop of the pale blue mountains.

Here and there cottontails scampered across the road to compete with the shaggy road runners. Strange little creatures that resembled field mice hopped across the road on their hind legs. We later found they were appropriately called, kangaroo rats.

A colorful array of hang-gliders decorated the roadside, waiting for the right thermal condition, poised for that perfect launch. When suddenly we arrived near a cluster of oak trees and turned right to face opened iron gates that seemed to invite us to what appeared to be private property in the middle of the National Forest.

We couldn't believe our eyes. We had just driven through four miles of high desert to find acres and acres of green pastures, studded with Spanish oaks. Well-graded roads connected the building sites, and an occasional animal grazed on new spring growth.

"This is too good to be true," Anne said, a catch in her voice.

"I feel the same. Who would have thought this existed on this mountaintop. Let's go and see what they have."

Elated to drive around at this higher elevation, made us eager to see more of this unique development. "There must be a sales office." My ecstatic spouse said.

Soon we saw a small red-roofed building near what appeared to be a man-made lake, and parked our car. Scattered about under a Monterey pine were several picnic tables with children playing nearby. Older ones paddled about on the lake in small skiffs while parents read colorful sales brochures. The clubhouse wasn't much, only one large room with adjoining baths at the rear.

"Gee, isn't this some place?" said John, our youngest. And with a gleeful look, John pushed a skiff into the lake.

I picked up a color pamphlet to see the prices. A map on the last page showed a 133-lot subdivision, most 2-1/2 acres or more.

"Are these lots large enough for you,?" Anne teased.

"Oh yes," I said, thinking it ideal size. "Are you sure you like it here?"

I noticed that three lots were designated as community property, possibly for parks and clubhouse. A brief history of the property told us that this was once an old Spanish land grant, used for many years as a mountain *portrero,* by a San Juan Capistrano family.

We glanced at each other with that knowing eagerness we both felt. Have we finally found our weekend Shangri-la, a unique place where we will build our retirement home?

Back in our station wagon. we happily drove off to choose our building site. On our way, I recalled that generally there are two types of dwellers, the "nesters" and the "perchers". Somehow we had always belonged to the latter. Not because of any illusions of grandeur, rather astronomy was one of my serious hobbies. To build an observatory for my telescope was one reason to distance ourselves from populated areas with city lights.

Our past experience with observatory sites was a good lesson in planning. We had built a lovely home on a hill above a quiet little town. With a single room on the third floor designed as a observatory. With a part of the roof which slid open for viewing the night sky. Here, we observed the mysterious night sky I had often wondered about in my youth. This room was also an escape from the trials of everyday living, to be alone and explore ones psyche, or at times paint portraits of my growing children.

One day the city fathers approved plans for a large shopping mall and extensive parking facility, with high-intensity lighting. In a few months the night sky glowed from the reflected city lights, obscuring most faint stars we had seen before. So much for our observatory near the city.

"Can you imagine the night sky at this elevation?" Anne asked, as we headed for the higher ground of the development.

Soon, we came to a cul-de-sac, near a beautiful knoll, littered with huge pink granite boulders. Around them, heavy sage brush and scrub oak covered the hill. Adding to this tranquil scene, century plants with their flowery heads popped up here and there, showing off their grandeur. A sign read "Site 56"; our brochure showed it had 3.3 acres and was still available.

We parked in a large area already graded by the developer, "What a great building pad this would make," I said, "even room for a tennis court, or an Olympic-size pool."

"More likely, an orchard would be better here." Said Anne.

After exploring the property for some time, we decided this was what we had searched for these many months.

"What do you think? Do you like this lot?"

"It certainly is unique; I still can't believe this place." She replied.

"The nice part: The developer has already graded our building pad." I said, as I visualized our classic style.

We returned to the clubhouse to make an offer. Much to our surprise, the salesman told us the lot was sold.

"Are you sure? Our brochure says it's for sale."

"Yes I am," the man said with an impatient smile. "Don't worry we have plenty of similar building sites around."

We looked at each other, hardly believing our ears. With our enthusiasm somewhat diminished, we reluctantly pushed on to look at more lots. But, we had seen the exact spot for our dream home on Lot 56. That enchanted knoll with pink granite boulders belonged to us, along with the manzanita trees and the flowered paths. We felt as if we had lost a dear friend.

"How could this happen to us?" I asked.

"I know how you must feel, but we'll find another." Said Anne.

As an experienced buyer, something occurred to me. "What if money had not been exchanged for the lot?" I asked, "After all, this is a new development. Let's drive down and ask the salesman?"

Sure enough, no money actually changed hands. "Mr. Bishop asked me to hold this lot till next weekend." Said the salesman. "But he didn't give a deposit."

"He'll be very disappointed next week." I said with a happy heart. "Under California law this lot is still available."

"No argument there, my friend." said he, "How much will you put down?"

I gave the nice old man a check for the down payment and a warm handshake. Back we went, to explore our beautiful lot, one we almost lost. We lucked out. It was a good idea to double-check with the salesman.

We soared on cloud nine and maintained that blessed altitude the rest of that day.

Our Enchanted Knoll

With the building plans in the station wagon we tried to position our proposed home on the knoll. This way, that way, until the readymade building pad decided on a north-south orientation. This would place our bedroom where the sunrise would greet us every leisurely day. With the large boulders on the west side, there was plenty of space for the 40 by 100-foot building pad. We had no tape measure, but stepping it off showed us we had enough for a small front yard next to the boulders.

"Just look at that breathtaking view," I said, pointing to the north. From the top of the knoll, and as far as the eye could see, appeared the same rolling hills, and small cities we had observed on our drive here.

"It's like another world," Anne remarked. "I still can't believe this is our lot,"

We suddenly felt spiritually bonded to this knoll, as if it was created for our time and just for us. We found later that the northwest view was to Los Angeles County, and the odd peak on the left was Saddleback Mountain, part of Orange County. This made four counties, or parts of, we could see from our new building site.

Our 14-year son old joined us after an afternoon of boating, "What do you think of our new place, John?" his mother asked.

"I like it, Mom. It's really neat here."

Another welcome feature was a flat acre on our property. Bull-dozed by the developer, for its decomposed granite.

"You're right! This is a good place for an orchard. But, would decomposed granitite be good for fruit trees?"

"I'm not sure, but if I know you, you'll find a way." Anne said.

In our mind's eye, we could picture the apricot, peach and almond trees, blooming in the spring. Exploring the eastern part of the lot, we found scattered a profusion of wild flowers of many colors. Here and there, rare manzanita trees popped up near our future building pad. Only one had to be moved to allow for the garage and drive.

"Let's stay until dark," I suggested. "I can't wait to see the night sky at this elevation."

To our amazement the early evening sky was unbelievably bright with galaxies and stars. At our former home, we had to wait till about nine PM before we could see stars. Here, after sunset, the sky looked as good as any three-hour astrophotography. Deep sky objects mixed with so many stars made it difficult to locate the constellations.

"Look at Sirius. It looks like a hanging chandelier," I said, pointing. Canes Major already low in the western sky. Comma Berenices popped out of the sky to the naked eye like never before.

"What a place for an observatory," I remarked. "A stargazer's paradise,"

Anne pointed a finger at me, and warned, "Remember, we build the house first."

As we got into our car to leave, I couldn't believe the fabulous events that transpired that day. Why did we leave our small telescope at home? But how could we have known that this beautiful spot existed when we left that morning? I suddenly felt a bit humble and unworthy of this new experience.

"Thank you, God, for this day." I whispered, pulling her to me and hugging her gently. Miles away, a million lights sparked like diamonds from the distant cities below. We disliked leaving this fascinating place. We both had an early wake-up in the morning, and retirement was still in the distant future for us. Tomorrow morning, the alarm clock would ring and today will seem as if it never happened.

Before we passed through the front gate, Anne suggested, "Let's check the mileage to see how far it is to La Habra?"

"Good idea, I'm curious too."

Our hearts sang as we drove down our magic mountain. We had finally bought the building site of our dreams, with a knoll ordained for our Romantic-classic style home. I thought what I would give to know of our future there. But then, it is best to leave such thoughts to fate. To know ones destiny would take all the fun out of living. I glanced at my wife's face, washed by the cool lights of the car's dash, and thought how good fate had been to us. When from the backseat came the typical question, "How soon will we be home?"

"In about 20 minutes, son." I

As I reflected on the day's events, I felt a presence of a new bond forming between us. I reached for Anne's hand. "Anymore days like this, and my heart won't be able to take it."

Her glance my direction, said she felt the same. Her remark however was uncalled for, "Honey, please build our dream home, before your heart gives out."

CHAPTER SEVEN

WORK YOU CAN DO

To ford a stream, one must chance wet feet—Anon

As we enter our middle years we pass a milestone of giving our best to our family, careers, and financial planning. Around the corner of the next few years lay the rewards of our efforts. We envision a more moderate way of life ahead, a less frantic pace of financial maneuvering and perhaps decide where we want to live. We also learn that any decisions made are not carved in stone, and can always be changed to suit the builder. The following are several that will depend mostly on your preferences, and cash flow:

1) An apartment in a suitable area, putting up with the neighbors' and the landlord's antics.
2) A mobile home, rent or buy the space.
3) A ready-built single or attached home in a retirement community with all the amenities.
4) Buy a suitable building site, and design a home with a separate suite to rent for extra income.
5) Design and build a retirement home in less costly areas, saving up to 45 percent by doing most of the work yourself.
6) Be your own general contractor, hire subs to build, and save up to 25 percent.

With options 4, 5, and 6, you have taken the first step to enhance your retirement. Option 6 will not save as much as you would in doing most of the building, but it will give you a delightful opportunity to design and supervise the construction of your home.

We enjoyed this experience twice, and can honestly say that building our home proved to be an exhilarating experience, one which has stayed with us to this day.

We visited many building supply stores, gather9ng vital information for the various construction phases. We also researched new building techniques and various materials. All this paid off in having less structural problems, plus a hefty saving in time and money.

Most general contractors charge by the square foot of living space; doing your own contracting, you could save up to 20 percent in building costs. The larger the home, the more money is saved. As a former home builder, I found that sometimes a compact home may cost as much per square foot to build, as a more spacious one. One must go through all the phases for a small house as for a larger one. I say, don't be afraid to splurge on yourself. Should the larger model with a guest-room please you, go for it, especially if you are doing most of the work. The little difference will only show in material costs.

Oddly, a builder can save more money on a two-story home, than a single floor model. By stacking and cutting the roof area by 50 percent. And so will electrical runs and heating ducts be shorter, along with plumbing pipes. You can also save 50 % on ceiling insulation. However tempting a two-story may be, common sense tells us, old-timers need a single story home.

Since most of us are good at something; we can save much more if we do some of the work. To carry this a bit further, the money we save, are funds we didn't have to borrow, or take from an interest-bearing trust fund. To borrow building money, the interest alone for the first year would be exorbitant.

Since no special skills are needed, anyone can build a home by using subcontractors. Before building our first home, we asked the city building department if we could draw our plans. I still remember the old-timer's remark. "This is America, a free country. You can build any kind of home as long as it meets municipal building codes. Do keep it simple," He added. "Otherwise you may have to hire a structural engineer to design complicated structures."

Construction know-how of every phase is easily obtained from books, building supply stores. It would be wise to check the book to see if it covers the different phases, such as foundation, framing and roofing. An example. I did all the electrical wiring in our first home with the help of a clearly illustrated 50-page book on house circuits.

I hope what I say will not discourage some readers. If still employed, and you want to build your home, allow five to six months time for the plans, permit, and plan inspection.

Read how-to books, and research the latest procedures, plus the availability of new building materials. All this information will allow you to build the best possible home, plus you'll save time and money.

Each home-building project has a different set of unpredictable problems to solve for the builder. Yet as I look back to our experience, we did not see some of the difficulties as problems, but as challenges to be met.

As many have never seen a home built, it is important for first-time builders to observe how different phases are done. From grading of the site, framing, roofing and plastering of the interior. By taking notes on all these construction phases you may compare the work of your own subcontractor when building begins. As mentioned earlier, I visited many building sites, with clip board, taking notes on finishing different phases without being questioned by the crew.

Working With Subs

Most subcontractors know their jobs, are honest, hard working, and rarely need to be watched on the job. Electrician, plumber, floor tile and grading subs may be one-man operations. All have a reputation to uphold; otherwise they soon would be out of a job. Some may recommend other reliable contractors to make your job easier. Our experience was very favorable the day our plumber raised questions about the framing contractor.

"Too many fire blocks, and wasting lumber." He remarked, unaware I did the framing. If building code mistakes occur on the job, and are later found by the building inspector, the sub will correct them without a hassle. Many ask for a percentage of the contract price when they begin, then more as material is bought and work progresses.

There is a side to contracting a builder should know. "Nothing can be more frustrating than having a disagreeable subcontractor." an associate once said. For this reason, an airtight contract is a must. An obstinate sub-contractor can delay construction for weeks, causing stress in a project that should be a once in a lifetime pleasure.

We were fortunate with the one we had. The same ones worked for our neighbors, where we had examined their work and spoke with the owners. We found most met reasonable demands, and all dealings were positive. Some may see us as too trusting, by taking risks while building Yet, this worked for us, because by placing trust in our hardworking subcontractors, they reacted in kind.

A verbal promise and friendly handshake were enough to get a subcontractor to do his job. I can remember the only time we had a written contract was with plumbing sub while building our first home. Oddly it was at his suggestion so there would be no misunderstanding about the quality of tubs, toilets and sinks we agreed on originally.

Building cost estimates are the most important factor for a good builder and contractor. If you underestimate material and labor costs, you may have to stop construction until more money is available. Although such a delay may not be serious, it certainly will be if you are using a bank construction loan. I realize this is scary, but sometimes, in a discrepancy, the loan officer will allow more funding, but at cost, by forcing the owner to hire a general contractor to finish the home.

Typically, we were impatient with the progress of our first home while working with our own money. The home was completely framed and roofed using money from rental income. Although we lived on the property, and were not pressed to complete the home. the slow pace of funds from our rentals caused us to borrow funds.

We had a momentary scare when a mortgage broker warned us, that no bank will loan money once, construction had begun. Luckily, my talk with our bank manager, funds were granted to complete our home. Why? The manager saw little risk, because we had practically build a 2,700 sq. foot home, using our money. All we needed was plastering the interior walls, and painting

It would be prudent to add 10 to 15 percent more to your original building cost estimate. A sudden inflation may cause problems, and most material bids are only good for 30 days. And, you may forget an item or a design change which may bring the cost higher.

Let's say, you have now selected a well-located building lot in a desired neighborhood. You are ready to apply for your building permit, and a foundation contractor is ready to grade the site. To make your job as trouble-free as possible, you should have also completed these steps:

1) Have ready cash, or a construction loan to pay subcontractors and building material suppliers.
2) Apply for liability, and fire risk insurance policy.
3) Visit the building and safety department for local codes and spec sheets. Check on zoning, setbacks, and the need for test borings.

4) Have about four copies of plans, two for the building department and the rest for you, and subcontractors.

5) Have plan-check completed and building permit from the department of building and safety.

6) Research all construction phases, by visiting other building sites.

7) Read available booklets on foundation, framing, roofing and drywall installation.

8) Choose subcontractors carefully before accepting bids.

9) Establish contact with building supply people for cost estimates.

10) Have complete cost-breakdown and specification sheets prepared. Even though you may use your own building funds such sheets are essential for first-time builders.

If all the above have been met, your job as owner-builder is commendable. You have done a huge part of your work, and the rest should be a pleasurable experience for you and your spouse.

When a building site is not too complicated, your foundation and slab contractor will also grade the site. These two jobs are well connected and you have one less contractor to worry about.

Make sure you call the building inspector before pouring concrete footing. Inspection for depth of foundation and steel used must be signed off on the building permit.

Visit the local electric power company about hooking up to a temporary meter. The subs will save time and effort when using the utilities' power. In the past we had used a generator for several months, and found there is nothing like the convenience of real amps from the utility company.

Although we did our own framing, these contractors are a special lot; their work is one of the most important phases of construction. Be sure to hire one who is well experienced. Newly licensed subs may have experience in remodeling, but may never have built a complete home. Speed is important in framing, especially in the rainy season. We could hardly wait to install the roof when we built our first home.

I've seen fully framed homes drying and splintering in the hot sun when construction stopped. Some framing contractors take on too many jobs in the building season, and can't finish all of them without damage to the lumber. Another builder failed to wrap the house when he lost his siding contractor, and had a hard time finding another. I would stipulate this in the framing contract: Once the framing has begun, it will be completed without interruption.

Don't get ahead of yourself in some construction phases. Phone your plumbing sub before you pour the footings. He can waste much time drilling through concrete walls to put in drain pipes.

Give your roofing contractor ample notice before the roof sheathing is completed, so there won't be delays in foul weather. Try to be present when the building inspector visits, and don't be afraid to ask questions. It is your home that's being built, and it should be built to your specifications.

Unless you do work on your home, it is not a good idea to be there all the time when a subcontractor is working. To some it may be a sign of mistrust. Do visit the site daily if possible and be near a telephone if they have questions. Keep in touch; a little praise goes a long way as we found out. A happy subcontractor will do better work.

Work You Can Do There are some jobs that even the least experienced owners can do, thus saving some of that precious retirement trust fund.

Insulation: Stapling the insulation in walls and rafters is easy. All you need is a $15 staple gun, and a safe ladder. Check prices of rock-wool insulation with several suppliers. Your family can help with this time-consuming work; assign a family member with good footing for ceilings and other high places. Ceramic tile is easy to lay. My suppliers were eager to instruct m on tile application. The satisfaction of doing it myself became a pleasurable experience.

Roofing: This is another place to save on labor costs, Most roofing bundles have clear instructions for installation methods. It is not hard to install a roof, but working on hot days, can be dangerous if you push yourself. Books on roofing give a general idea about installing metal flashing around chimney, roof valleys, and various roof covering. With such information, the owners can decide if they are capable of doing the work themselves. If questions come up, call the roofing supplier they are knowledgeable, and will be happy to help.

Electrical: Some of us are inept with a hammer and saw but excel in other areas. Consider doing your own electrical wiring if you are trained in electronics. The same principles and laws in ohms and resistance apply when rough-wiring a house. Use heavier gauge wire on extra long runs; we do not want to heat up the wall spaces with thin wire.

The building inspector will not stop you from wiring your own house just because you're not licensed. If the wiring passes inspection, he will sign it off. This does not mean that you can wire other homes. Again, you must check with your building department on this subject. If this type of work makes you uncomfortable, hire an electrician.

Home siding: If you do not plan to veneer your home with brick or stone, you can save money doing your own siding. Since most retirement homes are one story, it should be easy for even a non-carpenter. Horizontal tongue and groove siding takes a little more precision than do 4-by 8-foot vertical grooved plywood sheets. As owner you know your capabilities best. You can try a couple of sheets at the rear of the house to get experience. The secret of a good siding job, is to measure all work twice before cutting. If your work appears unsatisfactory, no harm is done; you can hire a carpenter to finish the job. Most siding contractors bid much lower on new homes. If you decide on aluminum, try installing some. If you feel like you have two left hands, have a professional install it.

Painting: All painters are not equal. Usually we had good luck, though watching one work on one of our rentals really upset us. He talked us into paying by the hour. After that, if we had painting to do, we paid by the job. Unless you have a two-story house, painting is an easy job for the owner and family.

Most paint stores bend over backwards to help with advice, and rent equipment at lower rates. Painting does not have to be rushed or become tiring. Should the surface need more coats you can do this later as a break from another job. This gives the owner-builder the feeling of involvement, which may be missed while acting as their own contractors.

Cleanup: This can be hard work for one person and should be tried only with family help. Know the location of the nearest dump, and the fees. A contractor with a skiploader could be helpful with large area cleanups.

Landscaping: After cleanup, this should be considered if the owners are artistic and like the challenge. We had always enjoyed these final touches of creativity and made this a crowning finale of our home building experience. Hire a landscape person if a green thumb does not become you.

Interior finishing: Some people would never attempt to build a house, yet they shine as cabinet makers, floor layers, and weekend decorators. Such owners are certainly suited to be their own contractors. They can hire subs for hard jobs then bathe in the glory of finishing the home themselves. This especially applies to those building that second home before retirement; there is no hurry in such an undertaking.

In summing up on self-contracting, I do not wish to imply that it is easy. Saving that much money seldom is. But you must remember this is your dream home, and everything you do to facilitate its completion will stay with you as fond memories for a long time. If owners have experience organizing projects in their jobs, or professions, they may find contracting not only as a way to save a lot of money, but challenging enough to make it all worth while.

CHAPTER EIGHT

HARMONY AND THE LAND

"If all mankind were to disappear, the world would regenerate back to the rich state of equilibrium that existed 10,000 years ago. If the insects were to vanish the environment would collapse" Written by Edward O. Wilson, entomologist and recipient of the National Medal of Science and the Pulitzer Prize/ He wrote this to emphasize how insignificant would be the loss of humanity to our planet.

Most environmentalists will agree that as the population expands into the rural areas, the necessity to disturb agricultural land can hardly be avoided. What were once miles of beautiful citrus groves and tranquil hamlets is now a vast expanse of industrial complexes and bedroom communities, creating traffic problems which at times challenge our sanity.

Newcomers ask how Orange County was named. My sad response: Years ago, both sides of the highways in Orange County were a vast orange and lemon groves. Driving the highway to San Diego with the smell of orange blossoms in the air is still a memorable experience for us. The many small towns that connected these groves were at times difficult to find. Now they are cities that have merged into one vast metropolis, completely erasing the citrus groves.

Very few developers had the sensitivity to realign the building lots to spare trees; their method to bulldoze, and strip the land completely to gain more building lots, thus completely obliterating the citrus orchards.

Our former area became the beehive of many light industries, thus making millionaires of land owners, and overnight created *nouveau-riche* developers. As a former farm lad, it pained me to see the land stripped of trees, and vegetation. In those days, such high profit oriented people seldom possessed the sensitivity to consider environmental issues.

At this writing, San Diego County is taking a developer to court because of an environmental infraction. He deviated from his original plan and bulldozed more than 40 mature oak trees from a proposed building tract. Some have been part of that landscape for hundreds of years. We hope this case sets a precedent for dealing with similar infractions.

To some my view on environment may seem contradictory, but these issues are profoundly important to me. I can't see a valid reason for a temporary owner of wooded land, to have the right to cut down trees that took 1,000 years to grow. How many of our human generations would that be; what strange law gives these people the right to destroy them? Trees that sheltered wildlife and provided shade for delicate flowers and plants should be given the same consideration as other living entities. We guarantee property owners the right to do with their land as they see fit, but what of the rights of these living plants? There should be guidelines and information given to land owners by county and state governments, to verbally inoculate them with enough human sensitivity to think twice before they destroy them.

Destruction of Our Forests: Though their needs were simple, our bold pioneers quickly built their homes from logs before winter set in. To clear the land and build with the timber was a vital step in survival, as was tilling the soil to provide food. Their prayers were answered with the onset of good weather and a bountiful harvest. We could hardly call them wasteful, or environmentally insensitive as their log cabins were built from wood, a by-product of land they cleared for farming.

Modern builders have no such excuse. A log home uses more than 700 percent more wood than a frame one. To destroy seven times more trees, should make us pause before choosing logs for building.

Since World War II our robust population growth created a need for millions of dwellings, further depleting our lush green forests. My last *Wilderness Society* issue shows that only five percent of the giant Sequoia forest remains. The lumber shipped from the Pacific Northwest to Japan and elsewhere must have broken a historical record for cutting down this precious commodity. On a recent morning TV program, an Oregon entrepreneur boasted of a new market in Japan. He makes big money exporting his precut log homes. This is no way to balance the trade deficit with Japan.

Our government is concerned about Third World countries destroying their forests, and possibly depleting Earth's ozone layer. What hypocrisy do we practice? A *Wilderness Society* article also said that the Bureau of Land Management uses millions of our tax dollars for roads to give lumber companies access to our trees. The sad conclusion, Uncle Sam may charge them as low as one dollar per tree, which are hauled on roads built by taxpayer funds.

The reckless clear-cutting of timber in the Pacific Northwest is a tragedy that we Americans must stop. There are owners who replant the faster growing variety, but how much future generation will it take to again see a replanted mature redwood? There is a way to avoid this: reduce the demand for such wood and promote the use of other materials. When I think of all the trees cut down to build our first framed home, I feel a pang of guilt. The most abundant material on Earth is sand and rock. Let us seriously ask: how would its use by the world population affect the forests and ozone layer?

Most of us love the look of wood on cabinets, floors, and furniture, but this represents only about 15 percent of the wood used in this country. It is the construction of frame, and log homes, that use up this vanishing treasure.

Builder's Responsibility

Experience shows us that we can build in an environmentally sensitive area without grossly disturbing its delicate balance and still not affect building costs. With imagination, most building sites are quite adaptable to any situation. A building publication show how a sensitive owner had Frank Lloyd Wright, bridge a creek to build a complete home. The heavy beamed bridge was its foundation. Undisturbed giant boulders and aspen trees added a final touch to the sensitive treatment of the site.

Before we graded our lot we made sure not to disturb the environmental essence of our beautiful knoll. This, the highest point on our property, where the home would sit, and with insightful landscaping will appear as if it had been there for centuries.

Our lot was not always covered by scrub oak and greasewood. Many years ago, large trees covered the area, till a giant forest fire destroyed them all. We found evidence of burned stumps up to 12 inches in diameter after we cleared a 30-foot fire safety perimeter around our home. Only the hardy manzanita, scrub oak, and grease-wood survived that fire. As this low brush covered two thirds of our property, we had to plant taller trees to complete our landscaping.

Nursery people told us that eucalyptus and pine do well in our locality and so do most fruit trees. Our concern was that some of the community was covered with giant oaks; how would they mix with other varieties?

"Not to worry," came their reply. "By the time the entire community is developed, owners will plant many varieties of trees. In a few years these they will blend naturally without being offensive to the eye."

On completion of our home, the cedar tree we planted reached to more than 30 feet. Our weeping willow, the nurseryman said, would never survive in our area. Four years later, it towered over our home, implying the grace of a southern mansion.

The maps from our developer proved a blessing for all the owners. Our plot drawing, except for its miniature size, was an exact copy of the original submitted to the Riverside County planning department. This had several advantages for the new buyer; it was very easy to duplicate and more important, showed the contours of the building site. The contours on the original drawing were in 10-foot increments, I preferred that our drawing indicated elevations in five-foot steps. The final drawing showed our building pad needed very little dozing, much less than the 300 cubic yards mentioned earlier.

The soil-test report was provided by the developer when he applied to the county for the original subdivision permit, and environmental-impact study.

Property Owner's First Meeting

Our first annual meeting of the Property Owners Association was on a sunny Saturday in June, with the developer as chairperson. About 30 percent of the lots had been sold of our more than 370-acre tract, and many issues were at stake. Anne and I were concerned about who would fill the new board seats, and the direction they would take, and how it will affect the environment of this beautiful community . . .

Fortunately, one of the early lot owners was an attorney, Garland Stephens, with him his lovely wife Virginia. With expertise in real estate law and their expressed concern for the environment, they were prime candidates to be our first board members of our association.

Several public officials attended that first meeting: a U.S. Forestry person, another from the sheriff's office, and some contractors and a utility official from Southern California Edison. They had been invited by our land developer and had particular interest in the development of our new community.

Police protection came up as a topic several times because of our isolated location and incomplete fencing. In every society group, a few people will cause problems. Hunters and four-wheel vehicle drivers had their share. With the proximity to the national forest, a few think the moment they step into it, civil laws do not apply. Some have damaged our properties with off-road vehicles, others shot out 'our No Shooting' signs even though shooting was allowed some distance from the community. The attending officer told us that police response time was about 30 minutes, sometimes much more.

The few disadvantages of country living brought to mind that the perfect place for retirement may exist only in our fantasy. For this reason I heartily suggest home builders camp out on their land before final agreements are signed.

Of particular interest to us was the bringing of electric lines to each building site. The reason quite obvious: We had suddenly pictured this beautiful community being crisscrossed with strung-up wires and utility poles. I raised my hand for recognition.

"I wish to bring up the question of underground utilities. As of now, all these oak-studded acres look beautiful and undisturbed. My question is, how will they appear strung up with ugly wire and utility poles? My wife and I strongly urge that we consider underground utilities."

Hands came up immediately. Someone asked the Edison official about the extra cost of going underground. His answer wasn't too promising; something about extra charges for trenching to individual building sites, then more for each owner to bring it from the street to the home.

Again, luck came our way as several owners took our position on this weighty question. After a long debate, underground utilities became the rule. Now it would be up to the board and architectural committee to enforce it.

The final decision: the tract developer and home owner's association would pay half each to bring the power to the lots, and owners would pay for trenching from the street to the individual building pads. Average cost at the time, about $400 for each, a small price we thought, to preserve the beauty of our community. Many have seen in the past, that 'get rich quick' tract developers ruined a beautiful area to save a few dollars.

That first year, much hard work went into forming a solid base for the new home owners association. We didn't envy the new board's position and were thankful for the time and effort they provided our new community

Permit Application, a Letdown.

Before building permits are issued, the owner had to get approval from the architectural committee. The builder could then take the plans to the planning department of the city or county.

About a month after we submitted our home plans we received a letter from the committee, stating that as presented, our plans were not acceptable. Our style of architecture did not mesh with the building proposed trend of the community, mostly 'farm style' and Cape Cod look.

We were appalled. We thought our home was perfect for our building site. Our reason for buying here was that we didn't want a community of tract homes that all looked similar, and Cape Cod did not appeal to us. This was Southern California, with a Spanish and Mediterranean heritage. How dare the committee impose their views and tastes on us?

Somewhat more composed, I wrote about our rejection to Garland Stephens, president of our association. I said that we didn't want to change the style of our retirement home, that our building pad would be about 200 feet from the street. With trees planted on the site, the home would not be that visible. Could the committee reconsider if we made some minor exterior changes? Garland's answer was not too encouraging. He did call a meeting of the architectural committee and some board members and asked us to present our argument.

What profound statement could we make to convince these people, our future neighbors that our home would not be a detriment to the community? Our building style goes back 2,500 years. Many of our southern states are dotted with neoclassic mansions. The Roman Vitruvius, father of architecture, first ruled that a building should have three attributes: stability, utility and beauty. Since beauty, they say, is in the eyes of the beholder, should a neighbor rule on our interpretation of it?

Final Approval

Speaking to the board members wasn't easy for me. This matter was close to us, and what a person wants to say doesn't always come out that way. A feeling of rejection loomed as we searched their faces for a glint of hope. After my statement, one hand come up. Our ranch superintendent, Sherm Chapin, stood to make a comment.

"I've been listening," He began. "and don't really understand too much about architectural styles. When these people first bought their lot, they presented their plans to the developer; everyone liked their home at that first meeting. Looking at their drawings again, their home looks very permanent." With a bit of emotion in his voice, he continued, "I want to say this: when all the farm and Cape Cod homes on this ranch turn to dust, the Salat's home will stand proud on that hill. Let them build their home and end this meeting tonight!" he added, with a gesture of his hand.

Everyone was silent. Has Sherm somehow turned the tide in our favor? Were they embarrassed to speak to us face to face? As chairman, Garland Stephens then closed the meeting.

We drove home in silence that night, wondering if our own interpretation of what a home should be was a bit off. As we pulled into our driveway, I glanced at my silent partner, "Do you think we'll ever build that home?" I asked. "It didn't look good for us at that meeting."

My rarely dejected wife glanced at me a moment, "We may have to sell our lot and build elsewhere,"

"There must be other tracts or developments that would accept our design." I answered gloomily.

Several days passed, when a letter from Garland said we had permission to build with the plans originally submitted, and to go ahead and apply for our building permit. I cast a glance at Anne Marie's smiling face, "It's ordeals like this that makes one wish for weekend retreats. Too bad ours is not yet built."

She hugged me affectionately, then pulled back, smiling. "This Irish Goddess is very happy you can now begin to build her temple."

Sure, we were elated with this small victory. Our neighbors loved us, after all. Well, maybe not love; perhaps they just tolerated us and our strange taste in architectural design.

The first weekday I could beg off from the office, we drove to the Riverside County building department for a plan check. All roads to successful home building are not paved with smooth stones as many home builders found. Yet such challenges make moving into them more pleasurable. With a sigh of relief, we realized this as a major step to the happy venture of building our weekend retreat.

Rural Challenge

We had found that wherever you build, there will be problems that are different and varied as you move further from the city and building supplies. Sub-contractors may demand more the farther they must travel. If the owner is not in a hurry, these costs drop considerably in the slow building season.

Though the nearest lumber yard was 10 miles from our site; this was not as much a problem as the delivery of ready-mixed concrete. The owner disliked our dirt road, especially after a heavy winter rain. Yet when we ordered our first 32 yards of concrete in the slow season, it was delivered without a grumble; perhaps licensed operators were obligated, and cash on delivery instead of construction loan vouchers may have helped some of our suppliers.

The laminated beam delivery was an unforeseen problem. Designed by a structural engineer, the 44-foot ridge beam would span our living room area and support the roof structure with its 18-foot rafters and heavy tile roof. We sent the specification sheets to the beam manufacturer who promised delivery in two weeks. But when it was ready, the owner of the 56-foot rig felt he could not maneuver the sharp turns our forest road. We promised an extra hazard fee to try, but he turned us down.

"This will be no loss to me,' he said. "Your beam is a popular size, and I could sell it to other builders,"

Back to the structural engineer for a new drawing and design. Two 22-foot sections of graduated steel beam were brought to our site, welded together on our living room floor, and lifted in place. Such unforeseen problems in building trades may occur to unwary owners and contractors. This could have been disastrous for a general contractor, unless he could assign his workers to some other job. Except for a three-week delay and several extra days to frame and plaster the steel beam, we chalked it up to experience.

Fortune smiled on us many times in other ways while building our second home. After the building permit came, word about our project traveled quickly. Contractors probably get that information from the department of building when permits are issued. One day while we cleared brush around our site, a man in a pickup approached our hill while my wife dashed from one bush to another in desperation trying to find the blouse she'd removed in the noon-day sun.

"Hi, my name is Jack. You really have some building site here," said a young man . . . "I own my dozer and do the work, so I can give lower bids on your grading."

We sensed his honesty and asked him the hourly rate. He quickly examined our building site and pad drawing, giving us a surprising low price. We shook hands on a verbal agreement. It may surprise many how helpful it can be to let their friends and business associates know of their building project. We needed a special art-deco item for our front pediment but couldn't find one. As I mentioned this to our postmaster I could see her eyes light up,

"I think I have what you're looking for, Andrew. A cast-iron fireplace screen showing the Goddes *Venus and Cupid in Flight.* "I'll bring it in to see if you like it."

I examined it closely, and found the surface very smooth for a sand casting, and the size was ideal for our front pediment. The 24-inch round plaque with high relief figures was well detailed. A ceramic supply store stocked the shredded rubber needed for the molds, allowing me to make the first casting. It came out so well I made several more just in case we wanted to carry the same theme to the interior.

While attending a party in our home, a guest asked about our building progress, "We're doing fine but the days are so short we can't get enough work done." I replied.

"No problem, my husband has an older generator he no longer needs"

The price was about a third of what a new one would cost. We could not refuse his kind offer and gave him a check. Months later, the Edison company gave us temporary power, and we traded the generator to another friend for labor.

"Why don't you drive to my place and pick up scaffolding I no longer need?" a friend asked at the same party. We graciously accepted Tony's kind offer and plastered our house that month.

Lumber prices vary from season to season. It is prudent to buy when prices are low That is, if you can cover the lumber and your site is safe from theft. Building in a gated community was in our favor. We received bids for our heavy rafters, forgot they were good for only 30 days, and lost when the price went up $400. Timing is very important in material purchases. Though you may not have begun construction, you can scout around for building material in special sales. In a local ad, a supplier offered unusual discounts on windows. We saved 25 percent over our lowest bid.

Your area may have a Builder's surplus type of store, in the yellow pages. Local contractors could have material they wish to dump at give-away prices. It is not inferior; it's just possible that he ordered too much or lost a contract to use it. Another approach would be to place ads in local papers for a special hard-to-find item to add a special touch to your home. An owner-builder should be constantly on the lookout for these special sales and liquidations. You may not be ready for the material and the purchase may appear illogical, but buy it anyway. It may amaze you to know how much you can save after several such purchases.

CHAPTER NINE

ESPECIALLY FOR THOSE DREAMING TO BUILD A MINI-VILLA

Attempts to define art, even in our time, are futile and often controversial. Some say art is nothing more than the reproduction of objects or ideas. Experts on human behavior may say that art is the only true expression of the human mind.

Pablo Picasso once said of his paintings: "The less they understood them the more they admired me. Through amusing myself with all these farces I became celebrated. But, when alone I do not have the effrontery to consider myself an artist."

Whether we call art an imitation of reality or an escape from it, most enjoy it to a certain degree, and can enhance their lives with little effort. When I first saw photos of prehistoric animal drawings on cave walls, I was sure those primitives never analyzed their motives. To this, I say, "Thank God for that. Some of those animals are now extinct; only the wall drawings prove their existence."

I earnestly believe that a hidden artist exists in all of us. Deep in our psyches, the desire to create artistic statements continually drives us, sometimes to pick up that crayon or paint brush, at others, a carving knife, or to make mud pies that may resemble an object. Many doodle in a phone directory, or note pad, creating a semblance of art. A possible hidden talent pervades our lives to some extent. Some of us take it more seriously and develop our skills to a higher degree at art schools, or may practice their artistic skills at home. With such dedication we can surely reach the point of expertise and be called artist. Most of us will never be successful enough to make a living at it, but can take pleasure to express our feelings by recreating objects as we see them and how they affect our philosophy.

Experiment in Design

Since my wife and I have designed our home to match our classic art collection, we had many hurdles to overcome. A multiple column porch, an ornate front architrave, and of course, a red tiled roof. Determined to make our dream come true, I decided to carve the decorative pieces for the many porch columns, and front pediment. These will be used to make rubber molds, from which many castings will be made. To enhance our home, we went along with the classic theme, and later cemented these to the architrave, column capitols, and roof fascias. A book on wood carving helped me much with a list of tools required, even showed various steps in carving. Soft woods like white pine and very sharp tools, makes carving easy, but time-consuming. I bought several pieces of 1-by-12-inch, white pine for carving. I cut them into 18 inch lengths for the trim, and began to carve the design I traced from my drawing. A couple of hours of this, and my impatient nature made me realize this was not an art form to my liking.

Necessity is the mother of invention. In my case it was impatience that made me find a faster and more accurate way to make this pattern. I used a one by eighteen inch pine board as a base to layer the olive leaf design in pieces. I cut them precisely on the table saw, using the angled guide, and attached them with tacks and glue.

Having sanded each symmetrical piece before gluing, I ended up with a finished pattern resembling a well-carved piece of wood. A final sanding and varnishing of the assembled piece prepared it fore casting for the rubber mold. Mu next thought made me pause: We'd have to cast 120 of these for the roof fascias. Later, a few more for the observatory trim.

Latex Molds

Which medium to use for the molds was a question quickly determined by the slow setting time of concrete, thus making multiple casting in a single day impossible. Once the cement set, we needed a flexible medium to easily remove the casting, even when undercuts exist. Plaster of Paris was cheap, sets up quickly, but is not durable for outside use. We chose the most durable substance in existence; concrete. But, with its slow-setting time, only one casting a day was possible. With the number of castings needed, we wanted a lasting mold that could be used many times. We chose the lasting qualities of latex, expensive but very durable for such a project. The nice part, latex can be again melted after one run, and used for a different design.

After checking out the needed items to reproduce sculptured objects in the library, we drove to a ceramic supply house to buy 50 pounds of shredded latex. Back at home, I used an electric double boiler roaster oven to melt the latex. Before melting, we also needed three quarts of good grade motor oil, and a single electric hot plate to preheat the wooden patterns and plaster mold supports before pouring.

In melting latex, one must not overheat the double boiler or the stuff will burn and become lumpy, resulting in poor quality castings. I filled the bottom part of the boiler with two quarts of motor oil, heating it to about 325 F to 350 F. In the top part of the boiler, we slowly added the shredded latex pellets.

This is a tedious process and should be done with care, preferably outdoors. The fumes from the very hot oil are vile and will smell up your garage with terrible or even harmful odor. Watch the thermometer closely and make certain that the latex will liquefy enough to pour smoothly over the pattern. Preheating the pattern slightly before pouring made a much smoother mold.

A while back I had designed a casting table on which a 1/4th horsepower electric motor was mounted, with a one inch pulley. To reduce the speed, a V-belt was connected to a four inch pulley, to which was bolted an off-center lead disk. Luckily, the slower spinning off-center disk caused the casting table to shake enough to level the wet cement for a perfect casting.

We could not wait to make the first casting. Before pouring, I fully understood the anxiety an artist experiences when a creative piece is to be unveiled.

Before each pour, a one inch wire mesh was used to reinforce each casting, resulting in a sturdy well detailed decorative piece. My mind had a relapse knowing all we needed was 119 more to complete the job. (More later on wire-mesh reinforcing when pouring the two-foot column sections.)

Should you want to retire in a Mini-Villa: Instructions Included?

If you're an ordinary Guy, Research, Research, Research. Draw your plans and submit them to your local Building Department. Woodcarving is needed to reproduce architectural trim. Latex is essential in reproducing your pieces, and so is a vibrating casting-table. Use half inch wire mesh to reinforce your castings. And lastly, a super-understanding partner is essential. Good Luck!

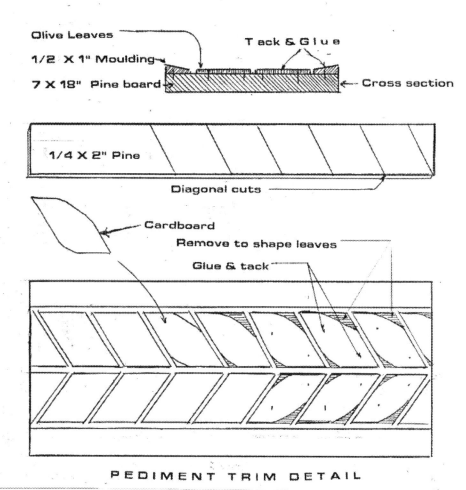

Olive Leaves
1/2 X 1" Moulding
7 X 18" Pine board
Tack & Glue
Cross section

1/4 X 2" Pine
Diagonal cuts

Cardboard
Remove to shape leaves
Glue & tack

PEDIMENT TRIM DETAIL

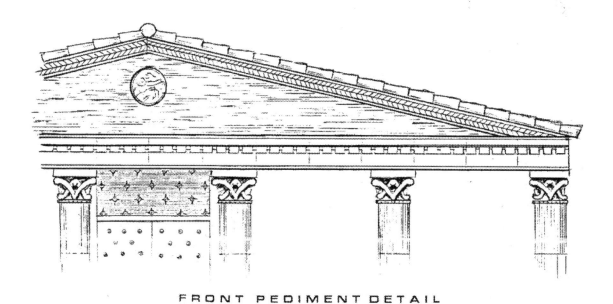

FRONT PEDIMENT DETAIL

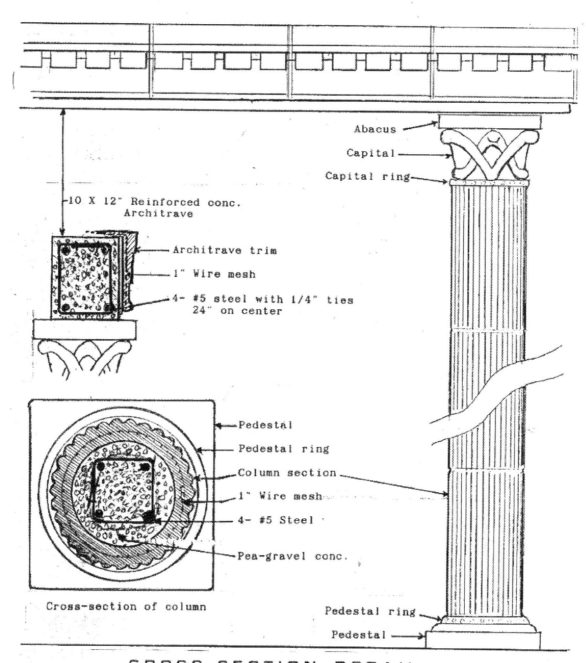

10 X 12" Reinforced conc.
Architrave

Architrave trim

1" Wire mesh

4- #5 steel with 1/4" ties
24" on center

Abacus

Capital

Capital ring

Pedestal

Pedestal ring

Column section

1" Wire mesh

4- #5 Steel

Pea-gravel conc.

Cross-section of column

Pedestal ring

Pedestal

CROSS-SECTION DETAIL
OF COLUMNS & ARCHITRAVE

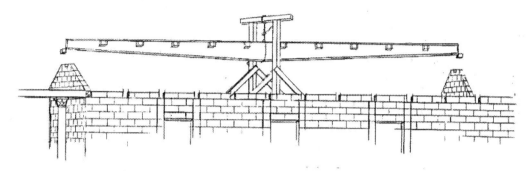

METHOD USED TO LIFT 44Ft. RIDGE BEAM

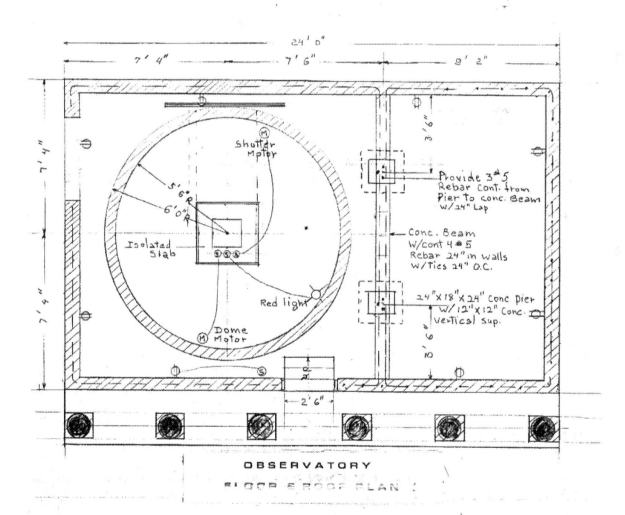

OBSERVATORY

FLOOR & ROOF PLAN

Pediment Trim

The front and rear pediment trim came much easier. This design was from a drawing of a *Temple of Artemis* pediment. A double row of olive leaves joined in the middle on the diagonal. Using the same technique as with the architrave trim, I cut a 7 by 18-inch pine, one-inch thick, then attached door-stop molding to top and bottom. (See illustration) I cut the diamond-shaped leaves from the same molding on the table saw. Layered and properly spaced on top of the pine board, they were glued and tacked to complete the pattern.

Each leaf was shaped with a sharp carving knife after the glue dried. I then sanded and varnished the pattern to complete the job. Now to pour the first mold.

Designing the capitols, column sections and pedestals took bit more effort. Jim, our eldest son, was in charge of concrete footing and slab work crew for a noted cement contractor. Son John, then attending a nearby community college, studied architecture. Both proved to be an invaluable source of information for our concrete and architectural projects. Jim told me about air-entrained concrete. By adding small amounts of detergent-type additive into the concrete mixture, the tiny bubbles formed allow the cement to flow easier for a smoother casting.

Later we used that same information on additives when we pumped concrete into the wall cells with pea gravel cement. The air-mix might also add small amount of insulation to the house walls, while the easy flow left little chance that some concrete block cells would be left unfilled.

Carving the Column Capitals

It took much forethought to design the capitals of the columns. We nearly settled on the Doric order for its clean lines and simplicity of carving. Still, I wanted something more original. After drawing several designs, none looked too appealing.

Events in our lives changed my thinking entirely when a phone call from my sister Ronnie informed us, that my father was seriously ill.

"It would be a good idea, to see Dad as soon as possible," Ronnie urged, "He's not well, and I'm worried."

The trip to Pennsylvania was thought provoking. As the eldest son, the idea of losing a parent dawned with a jarring realization. One feels helpless and profoundly aware of the implications. Even the building of our home has somehow lost its excitement and importance as we stepped off the plane.

To discover my Father in a coma, and dead a few hours later, devastated us. One aspect made his loss easier to take: He and I had spent some quality time together on a previous visit only months earlier.

On our return flight, my creative juices flowed again, and the idea for the capitals surfaced. Some say we do our best thinking at high altitudes. My father's first name was Adam and mother's Veronica. I simply superimposed the first letter of each name and had the design for the capitals. The sketch hastily made on the TWA napkin looked quite original but a little on the rococo side.

"What do you think of this?" I asked Anne. "Does this look good enough for our home?"

"I like it and it really does look original. Though a bit fancy, your parents are worth this honor."

This time the easy method with the table saw was out. I had to do some serious wood carving of this superimposed three-dimensional design. I had to keep in mind that the final casting had to be hollow to accept steel rods for reinforcing. Before casting the finished piece, I rolled a flexible plastic cylinder insert, 8 inches in diameter, 10 inches high, to be removed after the cement hardened,

Easy Columns

The pattern for the column sections would be 18 inched high, 13 in diameter. Anything larger would make the cylinder sections too heavy to handle. The final casting would have two-inch walls, created by inserting an 8-inch diameter plastic insert in the center before pouring. By luck, I found a 12-inch diameter wood column at a builder's surplus store, probably a remnant from a porch column. This was cut to a two-foot length, keeping in mind its concrete replica shouldn't weigh more than 30 pounds for easy handling.

Creating Vertical Flutes

I couldn't believe to have found such an easy solution. We glued and tacked lengthwise, 3/4-inch corner molding next to each other, completely around the cylinder for a fluted column effect.

The finished pattern looked impressive, but tacked on molding increased the diameter of the column by one-inch. Fine sanding and lacquering of the cylinder prepared the pattern for making the rubber mold. A plaster of Paris mold support was made, and when hardened, we melted more latex, preheated the mold support, and poured the first piece.

We made about four pieces the next few days, but as we stacked them I remembered the flaw in the design; the Greco column had a slight bulge about a third of the way up. To duplicate this we would need to make all five column sections slightly tapered in different diameters to create the bulge. The difference would be very small and the slightest error would be amplified to a large degree.

At the very start of designing we decided to follow an old Greek proverb: "Don't make everything too perfect, or you may anger the Gods."

What an easy excuse for our sloppiness. We made all the column sections the same diameter and our finished columns did not have a taper. Only the most fastidious students of classic architecture would notice. (Not really!) The gods were gratified, and that put us more at ease.

Later, we had a joyful thought; we can use the same molds and design when building the observatory. Though the two structures would be several hundred feet apart, they would match in design, but on a much smaller scale. Still, my preliminary sketch showed six columns in front of the domed building. This meant more castings to make, and more concrete blocks to lay. Oh well, let us not talk about this now. Building the main house will occupy our lives for some time.

To our surprise, we derived much satisfaction in designing and manufacturing our building material. This may have delayed construction by about six months, but this was no problem as time was not a priority; we had many years before retirement. We provided all the capitols and column sections for our neoclassic home by casting them in concrete in our back yard of our townhouse.

One day, our neighbor approached our fence. "Excuse me if what I say will offend you, but aren't you manufacturing in a residential zone?"

I gave him a worried look, trying to think of an appropriate response, "Yes, one can say we are, but you see, these products are not for resale; they're for our own use."

Except for the vibrating casting table, we made very little noise in our work. I asked him if he would please be patient a bit longer. The response was neither positive nor negative; we worried, thinking he might call city hall. Later, when they learned the castings would be columns for our home, our neighbors gave us their blessings.

Which says, honesty and the right answers, prove that people everywhere are basically good. We found the man was a pharmacist, and gladly brought our medical prescriptions for him to fill.

This was an unrushed and enjoyable time in our second home building experience. Though still employed, we found time to improve on original ideas, and carefully planned artistic details for our weekend retreat. The idea of planning and building a second home, long before retirement paid off for us. Playing the part of artists, dreaming up new designs and waiting for that first casting gave us a new insight to our projects. This can be more beguiling than the actual job of construction, and for a moment, we lost ourselves in just plain and joyous fun . . . like the art of making mud pies, to bring out the child in us.

CHAPTER TEN

BLOCK CONSTRUCTION BEGINS

No matter how independent we may feel, in project whatever we take on, there is a time to back off a bit and seek reliable help. This certainly applies to owner-builders seeking that happy day of home completion. I don't know why I had this compulsion to do everything myself when we built our first home. Except for the plumbing and ceramic tile, we had built that entire home ourselves.

This changed when we began our second home. I was 12 years older and a bit wiser, no longer having to prove that I could build a house all by myself. We also had a labor pool to draw on. Jim, our eldest, worked as a foreman for a large construction company, and John, our youngest, began his studies in architecture. We were lucky with our sons in the building trades, and daughter Joan who had just returned from a European back-packing trip, all willing to help to build our dream home. When the time came to pour the footings and slab for the first level I made sure we had the necessary help.

One problem in building on weekends was getting supplies delivered. This particular Saturday, on December 9th, my fiftieth birthday, a delivery of ready-mixed concrete was needed for the first level tor footings, and slab. We ordered 32 cubic yards of concrete and it seemed that on this Saturday, everyone became a "week-end contractor". Because we waited impatiently till 3:30 in the afternoon for that first truck; Jim warned me about the difficulty of concrete setting up in cold weather. His one concern was a late delivery of this unstable substance, as nights at the 3,200-foot elevation can get quite cold. By evening, the slab still wasn't ready for a final finish trowel.

It was nearly seven o'clock and getting colder by the minute when we tried to finish the garage slab.

"There is too much moisture on the surface for the stuff to set up properly." Jim said as we tried to finish-trowel the surface

"It's going to take a bit longer in this cold." Said Sherm, our helper. Whenever someone in our community had some major task, Sherm Chapin, our ranch supervisor, was there to lend a helping hand. This likable man saved the day for us several times during our important building phases.

The only one prepared to do slab finishing, was our son Jim, "You people will be cold without boots." he chided as we danced in our wet shoes, trying to keep our feet warm. It was past eight in the evening before we finished scrubbing the cement from our tools.

Next morning, I sighed with relief when I found the slab turned out fine in spite of finishing in the cold night.

The County plan-check engineer had told us that typically, as owner builder, we had over-designed the footings under the columns. I asked if we could leave it that way, and he said it was all right but it might cost several cubic yards of concrete when pouring the main level foundation.

For the footings, living room and porch slab, we had to a pour a 1,600-square-foot area, a typical pour for average sized home, except this was a second pour for our split level home. The porches and living room with the footings took 45 cubic yards, and at the end we had receipts for 194 cubic yards of concrete for the extra deep footings for the colonnaded porch This included the observatory and driveways. We finally found why the ready-mixed concrete people loved us. We were building our home to last a thousand years, and used a lot of unnecessary concrete. To pour the main slab of the second level proved more challenging than the first. Several perimeter heating vents were to be imbedded in the concrete slab along the length of the 44 foot living room floor. The main supply vent was a 12-inch galvanized sheet metal tube, with 1-inch interior rock-wool insulation. From this, 8-inch insulated vents branched to each window and sliding glass door areas.

The idea of perimeter heating vents was good design scheme, except that while pouring overly wet concrete, they began to float to the surface. In desperation, we laid heavy objects on the vents to keep them below the slab level, and removed them before it set.

"It's a good thing your lot has a supply of stones," Jim joked as he piled on more rocks. A drier mix of concrete would have made it easier to pour over the heating ducts."

We blamed the cement truck operator for the wet cement. Laying the blame like this almost always makes the home builder feel better. The main level slab wasn't that successful. We had plenty of help, but needed more experienced trowel men. A cement contractor would charge much more but the finished job would be more to our liking. Jim saw me frown at the shallow water puddles that remained after we wetted down the slab,

"Don't worry," He said. "Next week, I'll lay down a thin coat of cement on top of the uneven areas."

Jim first used special concrete glue, then laid down a thin coat of fine cement over the low spots. When laying concrete slabs and footings we must keep in mind that concrete is a very permanent substance, and not take chances during the pour. Get the right kind of help. Can you imagine renting a jackhammer to correct such mistakes?

Block Walls

Sometimes what seemed like good thing going for us became an embarrassment. We needed a part-time mason, but to this depression era builder their union scale was a bit high.

Dave at the office where Anne worked, claimed he had experience laying concrete blocks, and wanted to help.

"Ask him to come this weekend," I said. "This may work out fine for both of us."

The next Saturday I asked John to run the gas-powered cement mixer and supply our new mason with mortar and blocks. That afternoon, I left work and headed for our mountain to see his progress. I couldn't believe my eyes. In seven hours, he had laid less than two courses of blocks. Thirty feet long. Trying to hide my disappointment, I asked, "How are you people doing this first day?"

"Not bad after a slow start" Our mason remarked. "The first course is most difficult to lay. It takes time setting up straight lines with string and measuring to make sure the walls are square. Sometimes corrections must be made for the uneven foundation for the first course of blocks.

I understood, and realized our friend did not do this all the time for a living; I should allow him time to warm up and the process will come back to him. This was the lower part of our split-level home, where the garage, guest room and wine cellar would be situated. If there were mistakes, no big deal; plastering the masonry wall would cover them.

The next day, Sunday, our drive up the mountain was pleasantly invigorating on this winter day. The higher elevation of our building site made it much cooler than the coastal area we lived in.

As we approached the site, we had high hopes of seeing much progress by our two men.

"How is everything?" I asked our workers while examining the walls. After an effort at some small talk, I noticed some courses of blocks were not too vertical; while others areas showed a mild roller-coaster effect. I am not a mason, but I saw that all was not well. But, how do we tell a friend that his job is not up to par?

We had a sensitive problem here. Anne and I excused ourselves, on pretense to survey our acres, and sat under a Manzanita tree to ponder the situation. We discovered miniature white flowers poking their heads out of the fertile ground, and as I picked the tiny plant and offered it to Anne, I asked, "How they survived the night's frost?"

"These were a beginning of a mesmerizing collection of wild flowers that come up later in the spring," She replied. "Last year I used up a roll of color film on the flowered paths of our beautiful building site.

To return to our present dilemma, I asked, "What do you think of our new mason's work?" Feeling somewhat responsible, my thoughtful spouse gazed at the distant mountains, "I am disappointed with this as you are, but what can we do? After all, even though he is not my boss, I see him daily at work."

An idea came to me, perhaps a way out. "Let's not tell our friend anything today," I said.

"Tonight, when we get home, I'll do some mathematics to see how much it will cost us to keep him, and find some way to tell him to improve his work."

Using the figures the concrete-block company gave us, we would need some 8,500 blocks, not counting the observatory structure. The totals should not have surprised us. I'm not sure why I didn't see them before. Perhaps the variety of blocks used was just a jumble of figures to me, and this friendly block company, with no qualms about delivering up this mountain, gave us the best bid. Should we just tell our friend that we did some calculations and found we could not afford his kind offer of help? Hoping it wouldn't offend, that is what Anne told him the following week.

After that, before we accepted help from friends, we made sure they had the experience. It's easy to instruct hired help, but to tell friends that their work is not up to par is different.

Remember Electrical Outlets

We asked our building department, as owner-builders, if we could do our own electrical wiring. He gave me a quizzical look, then one to my wife, "Yes you can as long as it passes our inspection."

When home plans call for an all electric kitchen, air conditioning, and water heater, it would be wise to install a 200 Amp service box. Electrical needs usually increase as we add appliances. We can never have too much of electricity in a modern home. A 200-ampere box should be sufficient for most needs.

When building with concrete blocks we must keep in mind as we progress, the insertion of plumbing and electrical conduit in the block walls. It would be a nuisance to call an electrician every time we needed to do this. Most of the time it is easier for the owner to do it. We can always call an electrician later, should we decide to have the job finished professionally.

It is important to place the metal conduit before the third course of blocks is laid. This puts the electrical wall receptacle about 16 inches above the floor. We used a 3/4-inch conduit and bigger receptacles on some runs. To pull the electrical wires in the smaller half inch conduit can be troublesome, the larger size makes the job much easier, and the receptacle boxes simpler to hook up.

Reinforcing With Steel Rods

We already had 3/4 steel rods imbedded in concrete footings, but had to constantly remember to place the 1/2-inch horizontal steel bars every three courses (2 feet) when laying blocks. Checking the blueprints occasionally really pays off. This we did not do; since we designed the home and drew the plans, we thought we knew everything.

One beautiful summer day, my son John and I put down blocks at a break-neck speed to the musical beat of our portable radio, when John asked,

"Dad, did we put the steel in the second course of blocks?"

Surprised, and a bit annoyed, I said, "Don't tell me you forgot again?" I asked, trying to cover up my own forgetfulness. Lucky for us, we had to remove only about 20 blocks to correct our mistake.

To insert 3/4 inch vertical steel bars every 16 inches is the other item to remember before pouring the cells. This wasn't that critical since we could do it later, before the pea-gravel cement was pumped into the block cells.

Considering all our masonry work, laying concrete blocks was not that difficult. As you progress along in block laying and use scaffolding to reach the higher levels, a feeling of joyous accomplishment brings you closer to that last course, that wonderful moment when you are ready to pump the cells with concrete, and start building the roof over your beautiful home.

"What do you think of a time capsule in the corner block, honey?" I asked Anne one day. "Why not? They do it in all important buildings, and this one is certainly important to us."

We gathered photos, family mementos, clippings of current events and wrote a two-page letter, explaining why we built the house and its purpose in our lives. We placed all these items in a military-surplus waterproof container. I then removed the center divider portion of the concrete block for more space for the longer capsule. This was laid as the cornerstone in the southwest part of the living room. There was no ceremony, no speeches. It was a weekday afternoon, and I was alone. Only Smiley our terrier wagged his tail as he watched me lay our historic cornerstone, "What do you think, Smiley? Will our time capsule be ever found?" I asked our perpetually happy dog. His attention span vanished suddenly as a cottontail scampered down our drive. Oh well . . . what can one expect talking to a fickle dog?

An unusual and vivid dream came to me that night. It placed me thousands of years in the future, showing that a cataclysmic event destroyed our planet Earth. I saw pieces of our home, columns and capitols, drifting aimlessly through space. One tumbling piece, the corner stone with our time capsule, sends a message to creatures of other suns. It describes the origin and approximate location of a lovely blue-green planet with teeming life which actually existed eons of years ago . . . "Wake up Andy, wake up," Anne shook me gently, "You had a nightmare."

My return to reality was a blessing as I embraced her in thanks for her presence in that moment. A thought came to me, "How insignificant we and our planet are . . . a mere micro-second of time as compared to the age of our expanding universe?"

"Go to sleep honey," Anne pleaded. "It's only two o'clock,"

And yet, we humans make such large plans to fulfill our supposed dreams . . . what in the world did I eat last night?

The colonnaded porch would have been a challenge for most masons. After we correctly spaced the pedestals over the four #5 steel bars that protruded from the porch slab, we cemented them in place. Laying the two-foot concrete column sections had to be done a course at a time, with a day in between. After one try, the movement of the heavy pieces on the wet mortar caused them to slip from a true vertical position.

Our Greek Ruins?

The unique location of our building site with its inspiring view usually provided a gentle breeze in which to work. One summer day I laid blocks without my favorite helper, only the music of my radio for a companion. The exterior walls and the porch columns were about half completed, giving our site a look of much hasty activity, when the sound of wheels on gravel told me I had company. I turned and saw a yellow Continental pull up our driveway. A man stepped out and slowly looked at our half finished home. Showing a quizzical look, he asked, "I hope you people are happy: I drove some 70 miles from Los Angeles to visit your building site just to discover that this is not the Greek ruins I thought it might be."

He then explained that his flights east, had brought him by our area several times, "I couldn't wait for my day off to see what the hell was going on," he said, a bit agitated.

Looking at the construction scene, I could understand his coming here. Seeing the site with the classic column section strewn about and concrete blocks all over the place, it certainly resembled a Greek ruin. His long drive caused me to ask, "You must be thirsty. would you like some Kool-Aid?"

"No thanks,! I have a flight tonight. But, before I go please tell me, what prompted you to build this type of home?"

"It's a long story. Mostly we had always admired this type of architecture and it goes well with our art collection."

He wished us luck in our classic building project, and back his limo, shook his head as he drove away.

After the column sections were laid up to the correct height, we put on the precast capitols we made earlier. With the #5 steel bars in place, we filled the columns with a rich mixture of concrete. We then made the forms for the architrave beam which would span the columns and tie them together. We used 2-by-12-inch rough-cut lumber for the forms; when completed they resembled a giant size rain gutter 12 inches deep and 10 inches wide. We placed four #5 steel bars in this wooden channel and used 1/4-inch ties every two feet to create a concrete beam to support the front pediment.

A Special Fireplace

There are many books available on fireplace building and design. Several in our library show fundamental designs and different configurations to suit most builders. Since most of the heat escapes up a chimney, very few designs have proven the wood burning fireplace to be efficient.

We found an efficient system in the old-fashioned pot bellied stove. A friend brought one over to temporarily heat our newly enclosed living area. He also brought long sections of flue with elbows to connect to our existing chimney. A short time after we lit the kindling, the heat of that little stove kept us at a good distance till we learned to control its burn. We were told the increased heat output was attained with the extra long flue and elbow. This gave me an idea for our fireplace.

Our fireplace design called for an efficient heat circulating steel insert with a fan blower. Before laying the blocks around it, I left a two-inch space between them and the steel unit with rock wool as insulator. For the front of the fireplace we used smaller slump stone block as facing. Again, installing metal conduit for the electric fan was nearly forgotten, as we seldom checked the house plans. This is common with owner-builders; it would be a good idea to refer to the plans more often to save time and avoid problems.

As we progressed with the interior slump-stone wall and reached the vented area above the fireplace, an idea that proved to be sound later surfaced. Above the damper, I made an opening in the chimney flue, 16 inches wide and 48 inches high. This would be tightly fitted with a #18 gauge copper sheet to radiate some of the heat back into the living room, instead of losing it to outside. Several vanes were fixed to the inside of the copper sheet to transfer heat to the interior for even more efficiency.

"I have just the copper plaque that will fit that niche," My spouse said.

"Which plaque?"

"The one with one with the Roman soldiers on horseback?"

"That's the one." We never knew how much heat we saved, because these loving weekend builders were hardly equipped or well versed in the ways of scientific testing.

The Pause That Refreshes

With the outside walls halfway completed, we decided we needed a break from building. Our idea of fun when building was to hunt for antiques and rummage through salvage yards for decorative items for our new home. Our favorite place and a collector's paradise was the city of Pasadena. There must have been 15 to 20 antique stores, and a salvage yard we often checked out for possible treasures.

The reason, many beautiful old homes had been torn down was to make room for the needed freeways. The result was a profusion of Victorian and late 19th-century, art deco objects that antique dealers snapped up, and sold even faster to hungry collectors.

We found fine pieces of colorful marble at the local wrecking yard that day, but the wide slabs would not fit in our station wagon. Anne already visualized this historic marble for our master bath, but a 70-mile delivery charge would be a bit costly even for marble lovers.

The stained-glass department intrigued my spouse, but the prices into five figures were sobering even for us spendthrifts. In a far corner I saw three smaller stained-glass pieces that we could possibly take not real antiques but reasonably priced. The three 16-by-24-inch pieces appeared to be made with random size and color that pleased the eye. My mind raced to find a place for them.

"What about the entry area," My eager wife asked.

I took a moment to picture them there, "Without a window, the entry will look dark and gloomy. You're right! A good place for them."

Pumping Concrete

It took us several more weeks to reach that wonderful moment when the last row of concrete blocks was laid at the 12-foot level of the exterior walls. We were ready to pour the architrave forms and all the cells in the block walls with concrete.

After inserting all the vertical steel rods in place, I called the building inspector to have him sign off the cell-pour. John and I took a day off and ordered the concrete delivered, and phoned the contractor with the cement pumper to be available that day. This time we wanted the trucks earlier. As we found in the past, weekends are too unpredictable for delivery.

I now believe the ready-mix people always service the close jobs first. Again, the first truck didn't arrive till about three in the afternoon, when suddenly snow began to fall. Could the next two trucks make it up this mountain? The driver of the second truck radioed the dispatcher to stop the last truck but it was too late; the driver was on his way. Snow or no snow, we would get all the cement we ordered. Snow in Southern California? Or would this day prove to be a validation of Murphy's Law?

To pump cement into a masonry wall is not easy, but a lot easier than hiring ten people to form a bucket line to the wall, and then lift the heavy buckets 12 feet to the top.

While standing high on a shaky scaffold, the cold wind bit into our faces as we struggled with a large diameter hose spurting concrete. An additive had been put in the pea gravel to help it travel down through the concrete cells. This hose is heavy when empty, try moving it from cell to cell as the pump runs, making sure that none spills over the wall.

This is not bad for a short time, but after 15 or 20 minutes you wish someone would take over. The three of us, John, Sherm, and I, took turns for about two hours in a moderate snow to do this very thing. Often we had to signal the pumper to stop while moving the hose to a new location. This was time-consuming and forced us again to work till nearly dark.

The young man manning the pump appeared to be of Mediterranean origin. I thought, what a coincidence. "Tell me, are you by chance of Greek nationality?"

"My grandparents came from Greece many years ago." He said. "Are you Greek too?"

"No I'm not, I just build Greek homes." By the time we had pumped the second truck, it snowed in earnest. Afraid of being stranded on the mountain, the pumper operator wanted to leave.

"No way." I told him. "Your boss wouldn't allow it, and we have a contract to finish the job." Then I teased, "Why don't you be a brave Greek, like the ones we read about in history books, and finish your job?"

That did it. He stuck it out till we finished. Sherm suggested he follow the cement mixer driver down the mountain in case he got lost.

We must emphasize again that the problems that may arise in home building are as unpredictable to a general contractor as to a first time home builder. It is not logical to assume that all conditions will be stable most times. A builder must be prepared for anything in all building phases. The challenges are there; how we accept them is up to the individual. Oddly we thrived on such challenges that building a home presented. The reward of moving into a new home at completion, certainly justified our efforts. An excerpt from one of my books says it well. "There is a wonderful power in honest work to develop latent energies and reveal a man to himself."—A. Maclaren

CHAPTER ELEVEN

THE BEST PART: CONSTRUCTION ENDS

When the laminated beam manufacturer canceled delivery, we wondered why he failed to check our forestry road before they began to make the costly beam. Though disappointed with the delay of several weeks to design a steel one, we found other work during the wait.

A local manufacturer delivered the two steel halves of our redesigned beam and welded them together on the living room floor. We set a date with the crane operator to lift the beam in place, but a few days before the lift, he called to say his crane had broken down.

What to do next? Look for another crane operator? Shades of a conspiracy crossed my mind. To lift a ridge beam in place is a pivotal phase in home building, as it supports all the roof rafters, which finally secures the home from the elements.

Thanks to Sherm Chapin, our good neighbors became aware of our problem and offered help. We bought a two ton Come along to lift the beam, and built a "sky-hook" contraption out of heavy timbers meant for rafters. With the promised help and a gallon of red wine, we threw a beam-lifting party.

What a mélange of nice people came to our place that evening. There was Sherm, a retired dam builder; Gene Holder, heating and air conditioning contractor; Bob Lange, manufacturer; and Garland Stephens, an attorney. Raising of the beam began by attaching a heavy chain to the very top of our timber structure. We jacked it up about four feet at a time with the Come along, propping it up after each lift. We repeated this several times until the position was reached where we could swing the massive beam over the masonry gables.

The trick was to maneuver the steel beam so that saddles welded on each end fit perfectly over the masonry gables. This would be a true test of a good mason. Would the beam saddles fit over the gables that were supposed to be 42 feet, 8 inches apart? On first try, I had to chisel away about one-fourth inch of the masonry gable; on the second, I held my breath as my neighbors carefully lowered the beam in place.

Cheers came from the audience below, as I scrambled down the ladder to offer wine to celebrate. Sherm lifted high his wineglass, "I'm glad the crane man didn't make it; Look at the fun we might have missed."

This type of neighborhood camaraderie was touching, reminiscent of the barn raising days when America was young.

Easy Rafters and Red-tiled Roof

It seemed like everything followed like clockwork after the massive ridge beam had been lowered in place. With our son's help, and a friend's borrowed Skip loader we put up all the heavy rafters that weekend. My pleasure came when I began to apply the 1-inch, 4-by 8 plywood sheathing atop the rafters, over which we placed one-inch rock-wool sheets for insulation. We finished by putting down 30-pound felt paper with tar on the seams to prevent leaks.

To finally have all the timbers, and plywood secured from the elements is the moment all builders wait for. Actually we felt a bit too secure, as several weeks later, a strong wind took a small section of the roofing paper, prompting us to call our roof tile contractor to finish the job. Happy as larks, Anne and I sat on our favorite boulder to watch as the two young men loaded the tile onto the roof. We cringed to imagine lifting the 31 squares (square = 100 square feet) of concrete roof tile on our shoulders, and climb ladders to the roof top. These two men along with their fork-lifts loaded all the heavy tile bundles on our roof in three hours. Be evening over half of our beautiful home was covered with red tiles. When finished the following day, we drove all over the ranch to see it from different angles, and liked what we saw,

"I hope our neighbors and the architectural committee approve," Anne said,

"I don't see why not. That tile roof makes our home." We almost took a vacation to get away from it all. But knowing how easy it would be from now on, I couldn't stop from pushing on to move up our completion date. I was sure Anne felt the same way.

I could sense her excitement when we discussed decorating ideas. Bedroom colors and bathroom tile seemed a popular subject at the time. Knowing in advance they would end up some shade of blue, I pretended to be interested.

Framing Interior Walls

What a welcome diversion to frame the bedroom partitions after all the cement blocks we laid. The two bedrooms and kitchen partitions would be stud walls (wood frame and drywall) rather than masonry. We did our own drywall work as the job was not large. One can hardly call us professionals, but after we mildly textured the walls, the taped and feathered seams disappear like magic. Drywall people are fast and a good one could do it all in two days. It took us about six, but we enjoyed it and felt a sense of accomplishment.

When done, we enjoyed Shopping for doors at our favorite builder's surplus as they had the largest selection in the area. There are many door manufacturers and competition keeps prices low. The ones we chose were made of acacia, and to my surprise the hardest wood I ever used. We had to sharpen the circular saw blade after cutting. Each door had four rows of six high relief panels that made them look hand carved. We were pleased with how well they blended with our classic theme.

The Welcome Plumber

Our community was not served with sewers, so we needed to locate the septic tank and leach field before, paving the driveways. To select a man for this was quite easy as almost everyone on our ranch used the same contractor.

Wally and his wife Florence, ran a nudist colony a few miles away, and had as a sideline in trenching and septic tank installation. Being close, his bids usually more competitive than those of other contractors. Before we started construction we asked him to locate the tank and leach field. He drew their location on our plot plan to make certain we could locate the tank for future pumping.

To be located on high ground with a good runoff gave us probably the best site for a leach field. The soil was a little sandy which is good, but in places a hard composition of decomposed granite prevailed and had to be broken up. This was not so for people in the lower part of the ranch, where problems came up after heavy rains. Soon we had the complete system installed, which we were assured would take care of a family of seven.

We now began to spend weekends at what we now smugly called our "country home". It became quite a bother to run a half a mile to the clubhouse to wash up and use rest rooms. For some unexplained reason we had somehow put off plumbing contractor bids till then, but now made it a priority.

Our neighbor Gene Holder could be called a modern Renaissance Man. Heating and air-conditioning his business, as were cement mason, electrical and carpentry. He laughed when I said we needed a plumbing contractor,

"You're talking to one," He said.

"Would you give us a bid?" I asked.

"Forget bids, you'll have to trust me." Gene laughed, then noticed my concerned expression. "OK, Andrew: How about cost plus ten percent,"

We've not seen a man work that fast before. In a matter days Gene put in all plumbing fixtures, and hooked them up the following weekend.

Gene did a excellent job on the plumbing but pushing to finish his own home, never finished our air conditioning.

Windows to Our World.

We made the large sliding glass door in the living room our first installation. This one gave us a breathtaking view through our colonnaded porch to the valleys, cities, and mountains to the north. We did not follow through with the original plan, but I strongly recommend that a builder use double-paned windows. In severe cold areas, triple would be better. It usually costs 30 to 40 percent more, but a payback in fuel savings in a couple of years is worth the extra cost.

To install windows and doors in masonry walls wasn't that difficult. We assembled the aluminum frame with the easy directions of the manufacturer, placed it in the door opening, and marked he holes with pencil. With the proper size masonry drill, we made holes for the lead shields that were to receive the frame screws. If the frame appeared much smaller than the opening, we used redwood shims and a level to make it true. I must admit it would have been easier on a wood framed home, where only wood screws are used. Still, we installed all 16 windows and 2 sliding doors in two weekends without problems.

We found that buying from a local manufacturer instead of national brands can save money. We support local industry and save on shipping charges, sometimes from cross-country.

It is an excellent idea to scan local building supply brochures for sales on windows. Many suppliers will give discounts to builders; so don't be afraid to ask. Prices may vary from 10 percent to 20 percent between suppliers.

We purchased many building materials before we needed them, knowing that later we may have to pay premium price. If you are a potential home builder with long-term plans and can save up to half on building material, do it! You will not regret it when the need for it arises. It may seem illogical to buy before construction begins, but the savings proves otherwise. Several times I've seen in classified ads that material was free for just taking it away.

The long-awaited front door installation was next, giving our home that near completion feeling, and finally secured it. The door's rough opening measured 5 feet 3 inches wide and 8 feet 3 inches high. This required two 30-by 96-inch doors, hardly a popular size, but available mostly for commercial use. This reminded us of the fantastic bronze doors we saw at a wrecking yard in Los Angeles. They looked like remnants of aTurn-of-the-century bank building, except for the high price we would have bought them. The owner asked $2,400 for both.

The two we finally selected and could afford were one of a kind, 30 by 95 inches and almost 2 inches thick. Though an inch short at the bottom, I knew a one inch bronze threshold would solve that problem. The solid core doors were laminated with natural looking walnut Formica, which suited us fine. We remembered our front entrance area suffered a dreadful driving wind and rain in the winter which could easily have damaged ordinary paneled doors we originally planned to order. We have no regrets now; the Formica doors proved more durable and looked well.

For door finish, we applied one inch bronze nails, staggered 6 inches apart for a heavy appearance. We then placed on each door at eye level, two enormous lion's-head door knockers, we had found at an antique store sale. Again it was luck to stumble on such special hardware before they are needed, as we had never seen such knockers before or since.

To protect the doors from the elements, I first sprayed them with clear urethane, and as a finishing touch, ordered custom-made, bronze finish screen doors, with removable panels. When through, the entrance doors were right for our Mediterranean style home, evoking compliments from visiting friends.

That evening was the first time our new home became completely secure, but my spouse was not satisfied, "Are you sure you chased all the bats out of the rafters before you closed the doors?" she asked.

"No, I'm not, but so far I haven't seen or heard our little winged pets buzzing about, and you know what? I'll miss those furry little creatures, but don't tell Ronnie I said that."

"No I won't. Without bats in our belfry, I'm sure your sister will stay a bit longer."

Kitchen Treatment

I often overdo my woodworking mania. We saw perfectly beautiful kitchen cabinets for reasonable prices. Did we buy them? Certainly not! I had this compelling desire to design and build our own. Beside my hobby to grind astronomical mirrors, and test them on stars, I enjoyed working with wood. Anne knew me well and would not try to stop from me from this time-consuming but enjoyable task. We looked at new cabinets for a particular wood finish. Then we're off to the lumberyard for the walnut veneer we finally chose. The prices of walnut surprised my spouse, "Are you sure you want to build the cabinets?"

With some fast pencil work I found that even with the high cost of walnut veneer, and 1/2-inch plywood for the backing and partitions, we would still save over 65 percent.

My enthusiasm however, waned when we priced the hardware for the door hinges and pulls. When I spotted the unusual spring-loaded, touch opening device, with my "anything new mania" I bought them. With the completion of the kitchen cabinets behind us, we installed and hooked up the electric stove and oven, and finished the pantry shelving for storage of canned foods.

Our excitement mounted as the power company turned on our electricity. Our completion of this wonderful weekend retreat appeared closer every day. Electrical outlets proved to be a blessing as they made the use of power tools in cabinetmaking much easier. Suddenly we no longer felt that we were camping; at least now we could get rid of the old generator.

Built-ins For Book-worms

With the electricity turned on and kitchen functional, we concentrated on other wood projects and more built-ins for the home. A built-in vanity in the master suite niche was important to Anne, and our large collection of books needed special book shelves. All this was in the original plans; when we found some carved oak molding, we detailed the built-ins with it. We had more than enough book shelves, so we filled them with knickknacks to make my collector spouse serenely happy.

We found the perfect place for high-fidelity components under the stage area. We had already imbedded metal conduits for speaker wires in the living room slab which ended at each corner of the entrance area to hookup theater speakers. If a listener sat near the components by the stage, the distance would be about 38 feet, more than enough to feel and hear a 50-cycle note. This is a bit difficult to achieve in an average sized living room.

The guest closet in the entry area was a must for our future parties. I joined this closet to the bookcase to make it appear as if it always belonged there. Here again, the carved oak molding had tied the bookcase and closet into one unit, and the Italian gold plated door pulls completed the classic theme for the front entry.

Stucco, the California Way

When the rains came the following winter, we noticed a disadvantage to a masonry home: Water seepage through exterior walls. Though we had plastered the interior, driving rain caused mild seepage in one small area in the living-room. It didn't hurt anything but it bothered us.

"Say, just what kind of a home did we built this time?" I asked my concerned wife.

"I don't worry," She said. "My genius husband can fix anything."

Our plan to stucco the outside after the spring rains was still intact, but suddenly I felt a bit lazy. I felt a needed a break was due since it had been almost two years since we began this home. Riverside's building department gave us an extension on our building permit. So, a building break we took, and guilt at this time would be the furthest emotion from my mind. We had certainly earned this shopping spree for decorator items. And besides, we probably saved $100,000 in building costs by doing our own.

Like many weekends before, this Sunday evening found us on the porch enjoying our country surroundings,

"Do we really want this as a weekend retreat?" Anne asked. "The sunsets are so beautiful on this mountain, I feel as if I'm on vacation."

"Yes, but have you seen stars last night? I wanted to drop everything and start work on the telescope."

Another sneaky thought reared its head. It is only 27 miles to my job in San Juan Capistrano. Do we have to wait five years before I retire? I'd better put an end to these ideas. The thought of commuting such distance may be hard to take. I glanced at the now flattened bright orange disk as it slowly disappeared behind the horizon, and suddenly knew Anne had similar feelings. On that fateful Sunday evening while bathed in the warm glow of a setting sun, two hopeless romantics agreed to live on that lovely mountain long before they retired.

Incident at the Reflection Pond

Spring came early that year and our small fruit orchard in full bloom, presented a lovely picture against a cloudless California sky. Then too, the runoff from a last rain filled our reflection pond, giving a home to a school of wiggly tadpoles.

This man-made reflection pond served its purpose well but did not hold water very long. While pruning the olive trees along our driveway, I decided to give our tadpole population more water, or their high hopes of becoming frogs would be dashed into the mud.

As I watched our precious commodity gush into the pond, I told myself not to forget later to turn off the faucet. Because we must irrigate much in the dry summer months, we try to save water in the spring.

I happily stopped at the workshop to work on my latest telescope project. Time flies when we enjoy a day off doing work we like best. At dusk, a call from the house, "Supper is ready" sounded great to a hungry hobbyist.

The next morning, my dutiful gardener began to water her newly planted daffodils, suddenly stopped and ran into kitchen. "Guess what? It must have rained last night. Our little lake is full."

It took me full ten seconds to regain my composure, and in shaky voice, "No, Sweetheart! It did not rain last night, but I want you to know we now have the most valuable tadpoles in southern California."

Suddenly I did not feel like finishing breakfast. I left the table and headed for the pond to turn off that gushing faucet. A glance at a school of happy tadpoles somehow made me smile. Expensive or not, we'll have many frogs this summer, and their croaking symphony in the evenings will most certainly be appreciated on the front porch.

Finishing With a Flair

We gave a party for our wedding anniversary and among the guests, a stucco contractor, Tony Aros, "Who is doing your stucco work?"

"I don't know yet. My boys and I had already plastered the inside."

"If you want, I have some old type wood scaffolding I no longer use. Come on down and help yourself to all you want.

I looked at my friend, thinking, even our anniversary party helped our building cause. Some months later, our home had stucco, and was ready to paint the exterior walls. We didn't want to use a color coat because of a leak in the living room wall. A color coat is stucco mixture with color added in, and is hardly considered waterproof.

Application of the stucco and texturing was not uniform on the exterior walls because several people did the work. Overall, the finished surface resembled what some call, Spanish lace, leaving the walls with an interesting finish. We used that old excuse again: making it too perfect might anger the Gods.

A Change in the Plans

We moved into our home appropriately on Thanksgiving week, almost two years after we broke ground. This was much sooner than planned, but few can predict the move in date of an owner built home. I've been told that one can build a masonry house as quickly as a wood frame one, depending on how much help the owner can afford. We never regretted our choice of building material, and enjoyed the permanence of masonry our home offered.

Many times we hear the saying: "Let's play it by ear." I think this applies when building a second home before you retire. We really did plan our home as a weekend retreat, but as nature lovers, we were somewhat captivated by our mountain locale, and could hardly resist the urge to make it our permanent home. It had now become our island in the sky, and at times, the *Shangri-la* that most search for.

It would be prudent for those in their middle years not to chisel all their decisions in stone; be flexible in your options before retirement. Keep in mind however, although the perfect place to retire does not really exist, the one you choose may come very close to the paradise we all search for. Before closing a deal on a building site, take a week off and camp out in the area to try it out. One can learn more that way than with brief visits to the site, or broker controlled excursions.

Our lot purchase was never at risk as land values in southern California nearly doubled. When we began construction three years later, our lot already increased in value by 50 percent. What really hooked us on our area while building, was to camp there on weekends, plant trees, clear paths, and lay out future gardens. Not once in that time had we any doubt about our choice. On the contrary, many happenings there only made us love the place more as we prepared for building.

When time came to select the exterior paint color, we remembered our past scuffle with the architectural committee. Instead of the typically Mediterranean off-white, we settled for a subdued warm beige to match the nearby granite boulders. This was a good choice, and after painting the exterior, we drove around the ranch to see our finished home from several locations.

We also noted some of the fast-growing trees planted before construction made the place look as though it has been there for years. A large weeping willow gracefully draped over the collimated porch, giving it the look of permanence that we had long strived for. We could almost visualize this home on a distant Aegean hill in ancient Greece, for a moment nearly forgetting this was our enchanted knoll on a California mountain.

CHAPTER TWELVE

INTERIOR DECOR: AN EVOLVING TREND

Attempts to define art in our time are futile and often controversial. Some say art is nothing more than the reproduction of objects or ideas. Experts on human behavior may say that art is the only true expression of the human mind.

Pablo Picasso once said of his paintings: "The less they understood them the more they admired me. Through amusing myself with all these farces I became celebrated. But, when I am alone I do not have the effrontery to consider myself an artist."

Whether we call art an imitation of reality or an escape from it, most enjoy it to a certain degree, and can enhance their lives by owning art. When I first saw prehistoric animal drawings on cave walls, I was sure those primitives never analyzed their motives. I say, "Thank God for that. Some of those creatures are now extinct; only the wall drawings tell us their story and prove their existence."

I earnestly believe that a hidden artist exists in all of us. Deep in our psyches, the desire to create artistic statements continually drives us. Sometimes to pick up that crayon or paint brush, at others, a carving knife, or use clay to create an artistic statement. Many of us doodle in a phone directory, or note pad, creating a semblance of art. This hidden talent pervades our lives to some extent, where some of us take it more seriously and develop our skills to a higher plateau at art schools or practice our artistic skills at home. With such dedication we can surely reach the point of expertise, some call art. Most of us will never be successful enough to make a living at it, but can take pleasure to express our feelings by recreating objects as we see them and how they affect our philosophy.

Experiment in Design

With such thinking, I decided to carve the decorative pieces from which we would make molds for casting. When completed, to enhance the Romantic-classic theme, we'd later cement these to the architrave to connect the columns and roof fascias.

A book on wood carving helped me much with a list of tools required, then showed various steps in carving. Soft woods like white pine, and extra sharp tools makes carving easy, but time-consuming. I bought several pieces of 1-by-12-inch, four-foot long pine for carving. I cut them into 18 inch lengths for the trim, and began to carve the design I had traced from my drawing. A couple of hours of this, and my impatient nature made me realize this was not an art form to my liking.

Necessity is the mother of invention. In my case it was impatience that made me find a faster and more accurate way to recreate the pattern for architrave trim. I used an 18 inch pine-board as a base to layer the design in pieces. I cut them precisely on the table saw, using the angled guide and attached them to the base with glue and tacks.

After sanding each piece, I had a finished pattern for the roof fascia. A final sanding and varnishing of the assembled piece prepared it for the rubber mold. Checking my preliminary drawing, we'd have to cast 120 to cover the roof fascias, and a few more for the observatory.

The Essential Latex Molds

Which medium to use for the molds was a question quickly determined by the slow setting time of concrete, thus making multiple casting in one day improbable. We needed a flexible medium, to easily remove the casting before the cement is set. This allows frequent dumping of the castings. Plaster of Paris is the least costly but is not flexible and is impossible to separate if undercuts exist. With the number of castings needed, we wanted a lasting mold that could be used many times, with shorter time between each. We chose the lasting qualities of latex, expensive but very durable for such a project. It can be melted after one run, and used again for the next design.

After checking out the needed items to reproduce sculptured objects in the library, we drove to a ceramic supply house to buy 50 pounds of shredded rubber. A used electric double-roaster oven. As luck would have it, we found one in a secondhand store for only a few dollars. We also needed three quarts of good grade motor oil, and a single electric hot plate to preheat the wooden patterns and plaster mold supports before pouring.

In melting rubber one must not overheat the double boiler or the rubber will burn and become lumpy, resulting in poor quality castings. I filled the bottom part of the boiler with two quarts of motor oil, heating it to about 325 F to 350 F. In the top part we slowly added the shredded rubber pellets. This is a tedious process and should be done with care, preferably outdoors. The fumes from the very hot oil are vile and will smell up your garage with terrible or even harmful odor. Watch the thermometer closely and make certain that the rubber will liquefy enough to pour smoothly over the pattern. Preheating the pattern slightly before pouring made a much smoother mold. I now fully understood the anxiety an artist experiences when a creative piece is to be unveiled. We could not wait to make the first casting. I had designed a casting table on which a one-fourth horsepower electric motor was bolted. To reduce the speed, a V-belt was connected to a four-inch pulley. To the larger pulley, I mounted an off-center lead disk. The table vibrated enough to level the cement in the mold and filled every nook and cranny for a fine casting every time.

Before each pour we imbedded a one inch wire mesh to reinforce each casting, resulting in a sturdy well-detailed piece of decorative building material. All we needed was 119 more to complete the job. More later on reinforcing when making the two-foot column sections.

Pediment Trim

The front and rear pediment trim came from a drawing of a Temple of Artemis, and seemed appropriate. A double row of olive leaves joined in the middle on the diagonal. Using the same technique as with the architrave trim, I cut a 7 by 18-inch pine, one inch thick, and attached door stop molding to top and bottom. Taking a ¼ inch by two inch wide piece of pine, I set the table saw and cut the diamond shaped leaves, and layered them on the pine board. Using wood glue, I tacked each piece to the board to complete the pattern.

After the glue had dried, I form each leaf with a sharp knife, fine-sand the edges, varnish the piece, made it ready for casting. We lucked out again; the casting resembled to the original drawing in the book. Designing the capitols, column sections and pedestals required more effort. Jim, my eldest is in charge of concrete footing and slab work for a noted cement contractor. Son John, was then attending college, majoring in architecture. Both proved to be an invaluable source of information for our concrete and architectural projects.

Jim informed me about the use of detergent in concrete used in pouring concrete block cells. By adding small amounts of detergent-type additive into the concrete mixture, the tiny bubbles formed allow the cement to flow easier, filling all the crevices. The same mixture is also used in casting, resulting in a flawless reproduction. The detergent mix might also add small amount of insulation to the house walls.

Carving the Capitals

It took much forethought to design the capitals of the columns. We nearly settled on the simple Doric order for its clean lines, and simplicity of carving. Typically, we wanted something more original, and after several drawings, none looked too appealing.

Events in our lives however changed my thinking entirely with a phone call from my sister Ronnie, who informed us that my father was seriously ill.

"It would be a good idea, to see Dad as soon as possible,"

The trip to Pennsylvania was thought provoking. As the eldest son, the idea of losing a parent dawned with a jarring realization. One feels helpless and profoundly aware of the implications. Suddenly, our building of our home has somehow lost its importance as we stepped off the plane.

If finding that Dad was in a coma stunned me, his death a few hours after we arrived, nearly paralyzed me. One aspect made his loss easier to take: We had spent some quality time together on a previous visit some months earlier.

On our return flight, my creative juices began to flow. Was it possible we do our best thinking at high altitude? For some strange reason the idea for the capitals surfaced. My father's first name was Adam and mother's Veronica. I simply superimposed the first letter of each name and ended with the design for the capitals. The sketch hastily made on the TWA napkin looked quite original, but a little on the rococo side.

"What do you think of this?" I asked Anne. "Does this look good enough for our home?"

"I like it, and it really does look original. Though a bit fancy, your Mom and Dad are worth such an honor."

This time the easy method with the table saw was out. I had to do some serious wood carving of this superimposed three-dimensional design. (See drawing in this Chapter) I had to keep in mind that the final casting had to be hollow to accept steel rods for reinforcing. Before casting the finished piece, I rolled a flexible plastic cylinder insert, 8 inches in diameter, 10 inches high, to be removed after the cement hardened.

Easy Columns

The pattern for the column sections would be 24 inches high, 13 in diameter. Anything larger would make the cylinder sections too heavy to handle. The final casting would have two-inch walls, created by inserting an 8-inch diameter plastic insert in the center before pouring. By luck, I found a 12-inch diameter wood column at a building surplus store, probably a remnant from an old porch column. This was cut to two-foot lengths to keep in mind its concrete replica shouldn't weigh more than 30 pounds for easy handling.

Creating a Fluted Column.

I couldn't believe to have thought of such an easy solution. We glued and tacked length-wise, 3/4-inch corner molding next to each other, completely around the cylinder for a fluted column effect.

The finished pattern looked impressive, but the added molding increased the diameter of the column by one inch. Fine sanding and lacquering, prepared the piece for making the latex mold. A plaster of Paris mold support was made, and when dried, we melted more latex, preheated the mold and support, and then poured the melted latex for first piece.

What a great feeling to dump the mold, and see a perfectly finished two-foot cylinder for our column. We cast four more, and temporarily stacked them on each other. All we needed were the pedestals and capitols to imagine our completed column.

Stepping back, I however saw a flaw in the design; The Greek column had a sleight bulge about a third of the way up. To duplicate this, we'd need to make all five column sections in different diameters. The difference would be very small and the slightest error would be amplified to a large degree.

At the very start of our building, we decided to follow an old Greek proverb: "Don't make everything too perfect, or you may anger the Gods."

We made all the column sections the same diameter. And though our finished columns lacked a slight taper, only the most fastidious students of classic architecture would notice. (Not really!) The Gods however, were gratified, and that put us more at ease.

A joyful thought came to me: we can use the same molds and design when building the observatory. Though the two structures would be several hundred feet apart, they would match in design, but on a much smaller scale. My preliminary sketch shows six columns in front of the domed building. This meant more castings to make, and more blocks to lay. Oh well, let us not talk about this now. Building the main house will occupy our lives for some time.

To our surprise, we derived much satisfaction in designing and manufacturing our building material. This may have delayed construction by about six months, but this was no problem since we had some years before I retire.

All the capitols and column sections for our neoclassic home were cast in concrete in our back yard of our townhouse. One day, our neighbor approached our fence, with a serious look. "Excuse my asking, but are you aware that you are manufacturing in a residential zone?"

I gave him a worried look, trying to think of an appropriate response, "Yes, one can say we are, but you see, these products are not for resale; they're for our own use."

Except for the vibrating casting table, we made very little noise. I asked him if he would please be patient a bit longer. The response was neither positive nor negative; we worried, thinking he might call city hall. Later, when they learned the castings would be columns for our home, our neighbors gave us their blessings. Many times, honesty and the right answers prove that people everywhere are basically good. We found the man was a pharmacist, and gladly brought our medical prescriptions from his store.

This was an unrushed and enjoyable time in our second home building experience. Though still employed, we found time to improve on original ideas, and carefully planned artistic details for our weekend retreat. The idea of planning and building a second home, long before retirement paid off for us. Playing the part of artists, dreaming up new designs and waiting for that first casting gave us a new insight to our projects. This can be more beguiling than the actual job of construction, and for a moment, we lost ourselves in just plain and joyous fun . . . like the art of making mud pies, to bring out the child in us.

To visit homes of some people usually ends up as bland experience for me. We can study modern decorating at its optimum in some contemporary movie. One wonders whose home the set designers are trying to mimic, as some have a bizarre idea of what a home interior should be. The homey look and the family memento niche is conspicuously lacking in the cool contemporary environment of today. We'll, have to look long and hard to find Aunt Helen's photo, or one of a family group on the wall.

Sometimes I wonder, am I so stodgy as not to see the beauty in some of the art and music of this generation? Do my ears deceive me when I hear hard rock, with distortion amplifiers to destroy the nuance of a melody? How could I have lost touch with our fragmented society so quickly and where have I failed that I no longer understood its lifestyles and way out philosophies? Dare I look into the next century to behold what is in store for me? And what rules will future home decorators fracture in the name of something novel?

At times I feel as if had someone dropped me off onto an alien planet when I see some of our youth sport orange and green Mohawk haircuts, dangling earrings, and torn jeans. I'm no longer surprised to see a pretty girl with hair as if punished with an egg beater. Some of them want to be different and yet most are appropriately alike. The label has to be right for the moment, or their peers will not accept them as equals. What about the rugged individual stance we once held so dear in American society?

Some of this defiance is often seen in home decor. Though some refreshing themes prevail, most often new ideas are a rehash of the old. I've seen blank walls punctuated with abstract prints, off-white carpets randomly covered with synthetic fur rugs. Upholstered furniture is sometimes in stark black, sparsely placed and matched with square tables trimmed with chrome or brass. An occasional white or black arched bridge lamp stands over an easy chair, trimmed to match. Is all this to make a home feel warm and inviting? This is not the message that I receive.

For some, this may by a kind of rebellion against parental influence, and the home experience. Their singular goal was to challenge parental influence, and the home they can't wait to leave. To mimic their parent's values would somehow be an embarrassment when peers visit. They have their own declaration to make, and their own space to create and occupy.

Yet, as these kids mature, and gain the experience of having a past, like us, they no doubt will gather mementos, and may display them as their parents did before them. Let us not give up entirely on our present generation. To be different and mime each other is part of growing, something they must travel through, across and over to experience their own uniqueness as they mature spiritually.

As I look back, we too may have been guilty of such transgression when we furnished our first home. I now wonder what our parents thought of our décor, and furniture of which we now see in second hand stores.

"Don't laugh, but this is the style we used for our first apartment." Anne teased.

"Did we really? Look over there; that one resembles our old coffee table," I pointed to the sharp-cornered bleached-oak piece.

The old notion of decorating a home once and then staying with it is no longer valid. We should at times change the style, colors, and textures of our surroundings, to more or less, make life more interesting. To redecorate can often change or improve how we see or relate with loved ones. Surface changes can do a lot in redecorating without losing family heirlooms. We need not throw out cherished pieces, or sell valuable art objects just to follow a new trend.

Nothing is more satisfying to a builder than the completion of the roof structure. and the installation of doors and windows. To secure the home, is a signal to relax a bit, stand back and enjoy the goals attained. From this point we plan the interior walls and their treatment, decide on textures, and make color decisions. Such ideas buzzed through our minds though decorating was still in the distant future.

Many of you may have experienced this when you rented, or bought your last home. You were not sure the deal would come through, but you mentally decorated the home, perhaps took a second look, and in your mind's eye, arranged your favorite furniture around to suit your fancy.

Once our home was secure, we took a building break and returned to our old pleasures of hunting for antiques, thumbed through magazines, and for ideas, visited model homes. What we looked for however, was not easy to find. Unlike today, classic settings appropriate for our new home were scarce. We did decide on wall textures and colors, while experimenting with plaster. I found a texture we liked, one that resembled what some call, Spanish lace. We've often seen it in a soft yellowish-beige.

When first designing the home we used pilasters at all window and door openings to break up the monotony of long walls. This gave the window and door openings the feel of thick house walls. The oversized living room was another interesting challenge. "We don't want this to look like a barn, do we?" Anne asked.

"No, we don't," I replied, trying to picture the high ceiling, and immense wall areas we must change into a homey place. "But Honey, the large wall areas will vanish after we hang our paintings."

"Of course," Anne said, giving me a warm a hug. "I completely forgot the reason we decided to build a Greek mini-villa."

Once the home was closed in, I separate the entry from the living room, by placing two ten-foot columns, on pedestals, topped with capitols. The columns supported a decorative architrave, which connected the two outside walls.

This reduced the living room from 24 x 44, to 24 x36 feet. At the far end of the room, 12 steps down, led one to the garage, wine cellar, and maid's room. And six steps up, to 6-by-18-foot stage area, which led to the dining, kitchen and sleeping area of the third level. This move gave us a more realistic size living area.

I believe my wife and I had our biggest design dispute over the columns in the entry area. "The porch columns are beautiful. but why are you putting them in the living room?" she asked.

I knew she was angry, as she seldom called me Andrew. I shewed her the floor plan,

"Look, you can see them in the floor plan." I said. "These two black round marks are the entry columns?"

My woman claimed she had not noticed them before. Days later, after showing her photos of classic interiors in several mansions, Anne's approval came with a warm hug.

When designing a home, it's a good idea to discuss both exterior and interior details with your spouse. Make certain the drawings are precise, and well understood. Many husbands have their wives make decorating decisions. We agreed early in our marriage that since I too was sensitive to colors and space, we would combine our decorating talents. She could make all the decisions in the kitchen and master suite, but the living room would be a joint venture.

Ceiling Treatment—The Crown

We did not like our exposed rafters to be too prominent. The decision to paint them and the ceiling off-white was made early in our plans. Between the rafters, I wanted a decorative ceiling look, and attached carved hexagon frames, we found at a surplus building store. When I asked for 76 pieces, my spouse thought I lost my senses.

"What in the world will you do with that many frames?"

"Do you recall when I suggested a decorative ceiling look? These hexagons frames will do it." My woman reconsidered and decided I didn't need lobotomy after all.

In the center of each hexagon frame I placed a six-inch plaster casting of an eight-petal rosette. I drilled the center of each, and with a glue gun and a single two-inch screw, attached them to the center of each frame. The finished ceiling gave the appearance it had always been there and so did my stiff neck, but only for several days. The effort was worth it.

Blessed with a depression era mentality, but with Champaign tastes, we wondered how to light our spacious living room, and not spend a fortune. We thought of hanging a large chandelier in the middle, but the $1000 price stopped us. Instead, we purchased two 24" chandeliers, took them apart, and made one 36" in diameter. The salesman said, the Italian gold-plate fixtures were the most durable, and unlike brass finish, never tarnished.

We took them home, where I completely disassembled the two fixtures, elongated the main stem, drilled eight more half-inch holes in the main ball for a two-tier look. Carefully bent open, and gently repositioned the bottom tubing, to make the fixture 36 inches in diameter.

It took me a day to completely rewire the fixture and re-hang the crystals. The result, a much larger and more impressive chandelier hangs in our new living room. My spouse agreed that occasionally, depression-era mentality, and determination does pay off.

Reviving the Stencil

To visit Europe gives a person an entirely different slant in home decorating. We saw several new office buildings in Vienna with decorative exterior walls. It seems the architects there do not mind bending the rules of modern cubism. Most of the buildings in downtown Vienna are over several hundred years old. To mix stark cubism so prevalent in America and Japan would not fit there. Neither could we imagine such cubism in Prague with all its church towers. There now is serious debate in London about mixing such modern architecture with the old in that ancient city.

When in Rome we admired the colorful ceiling of our hotel and room, After a hectic day of airport customs, and Roman taxi drivers, lying down on our bed, and gazing up at the ceiling proved to be a blessed relief for us. The delicate pastel hues, along with colorful roses, mentally placed us in a serene garden. One could see that the artist was not a staunch perfectionist. Still, the delicate brush strokes created this feeling that everything in life is a misty dream, and reality was an illusion. For these two American tourist, it felt good to be alive, enjoying a culture of this ancient city.

If travel broadens one's mind, then it worked for us because we had some definite ideas to carry the classic theme throughout our new home. Many decorator manuals say it's OK to mix classic with modern or Oriental. But struck by the Mediterranean décor, we planned to carry it throughout our new home.

In our new home, nearly all our rooms had vaulted ceilings with exposed rafters. Our plan was to accent the area where the ceilings met the walls with an appropriate crown; I drew a couple of designs to be traced on the stencil. After several tries we had one that we thought an Italian decorator would choose. A mild arch, 7" high on each end, with grape leaves entwined with grape bunches, spaced equally in the stencil, and for accent a gold shield in the middle.

"What do you think?" I asked my curious observer.

"I like it. But how will you do the various colors in the stencil?"

"Easy! I cover the grape bunches and spray all the stems and leaves with avocado green. When done, I removed the masking tape, masked the leaves, and sprayed the grape bunches with purple."

"What about the gold shield in the middle?"

"I then uncover the shield, and mask everything, to spray-paint the gold shield."

Since I didn't want ragged edges, the stencil cutting was done with a sharp knife. After the intricate cutting was done, I sanded the edges, and masked the areas to be done last. Instead of a stippling brush, I applied the different colors, using spray cans of different colors, (See photo for results.)

One need not be an artist to make similar stencils. With patience, you can trace photographs or other drawings as long as the subject matter suits the intended scheme. We found stencil cutting a lot of fun and used it above the wainscoting on all the bathrooms walls.

Mural, Mural on the Wall

Looking at blank walls in our bedroom did not appeal to us. We had a colorful painting hung there, but the large empty area above wardrobe closets still bothered us. We wanted our built-in television in the middle of that area. It was easy to cut a section of wall for the opening to be later enhanced with a picture frame. Having the television installed that high made viewing while in bed easy.

We still felt we needed more in filling the vast space above the wardrobe closets, "How about a profusion of limbs with apple blossom to cover that upper wall?" I asked Anne.

She looked up to study my proposal, "Great! But won't that be a lot of work?"

This was all I needed to start preliminary sketches. After my Mate's approval, I spent the next two days on a ladder, making sketches on our bed room walls. Two weeks later, a cheery morning sun treated us to a wall filled with tree limbs filled with apple blossoms.

If I thought I was through, my fastidious spouse, found other areas that could use lighthearted mural treatment. One above my lady's powder room niche also got the apple blossom treatment. In the entry, above the front doors, I painted a six-foot arch with a gold border design. In the middle of this, we placed the leftover plaque of *Venus and Cupid in Flight*.

Floors in the Kitchen and Bath

We found a ceramic tile store with unusual imported tiles, including Italian glass mosaic. I recalled the many glass mosaic murals in Europe, and asked the salesman if he had more samples in the stockroom.

"If you are really interested in glass mosaic tile," Said the owner. "I have a selection in the back that will amaze you?"

Amazed, we purchased enough mosaic tile, for a large mural I had sketched for the front porch. We also bought the kitchen and bathroom floor tile. As owner, the man gave us a discount on our purchase.

Thanks to Anne's confidence in me, I could make these crazy buys without her questioning my judgment. A month later, I had a 5' x 7' glass mosaic mural embedded in the wall of our front porch. The theme: The Quest for Universal Knowledge.

We found west Los Angeles on Santa Monica Boulevard many stores selling collectables, and antiques. This time, however, we needed garden statuary and remembered a dealer that manufactured them in concrete. We bought several urns for our front porch and a large female figure with a lyre, a smaller one of the Four Seasons. I think we lost our heads that day and bought too many pieces, forgetting how heavy concrete statuary could be; our station wagon limped all the way home. On our arrival, my anxious spouse made a sign of the Cross, thankful we had no police citation for vehicle overloading.

As we look back, some of our escapades astonish us, and so did our exiting days of building, and decorating. One has to experience these occurrences to understand what we went through. We wonder at times, if the child in us will ever grow up. Is it possible that if we always behave this way, and won't ever grow old? Why in Heaven's name then, are we building this retirement home that only oldsters need? We found later that we didn't have enough hours in our days to do everything we wanted on those supposedly less frantic more leisurely retirement days.

CHAPTER THIRTEEN

THE OBSERVATORY

This chapter I dedicate to all loving and enduring spouses of such resolute hobbyists as I. Husbands who rarely know when to stop to smell the roses. Who sometimes forget to hug their children, or find time to expound their love to their super tolerable spouse.

One need not be a devout hobbyist to understand my fervent involvement in astronomy. Most of us have special interest we try to nurture to a degree of excellence, wondering at times if we had missed our calling. If some of my readers live with this transgression, please understand my folly.

Some amateur astronomers have no desire to build their own observatories. Others have never built a telescope, or would hardly consider to grind for hours, a super delicate curve into an astronomical mirror. They do not want to be involved in the mechanics of this fascinating endeavor. Their aim is to buckle down to the pure science of deep-sky observation, and delve into theoretical astrophysics of our universe. My dear wife Anne, no doubt may envy wives of such men.

My biggest transgression as hobbyist is my mundane curiosity for mechanical workings of the many telescope designs: Newtonian, Cassegrain, Refracting, Maksuto, Schmidt-Cassegrain, and more. If I had the time and resources, all the above would grace my humble observatory.

The bird watcher only needs the Audubon book, a good pair of binoculars, and a camera. A magnifying glass, and collector's albums would fulfill most stamp collectors' wishes. If only astronomy was that uncomplicated. In my lifetime I probably spent several hundred hours walking around a barrel to grind and polish a mirror to an accuracy of a millionth of an inch. And another hundred to test them on the bench, or a distant stars. Many hours were spent in reading books and periodicals on astrophysical theory, telescope making, and current discoveries. At times we must try mathematics to understand the movements of celestial objects. (Forget Boolean algebra. I'll never attempt that again.)

Some years ago, on third floor of out La Habra home, I made a 4-foot square roof opening in our ceiling to observe the night sky. Several years later, La Habra city fathers approved a shopping mall, whose bright lights destroyed my night sky, ending my heavenly exploration.

This will not happen at our retirement home. With an altitude of 2,200 feet, and miles away from city light, I'll be able to view heavenly objects never dreamed of. So, instead of a roof opening in the attic above our kitchen, why don't I built a real observatory, with a rotating dome, and working shutters.

If I use the left over cement blocks and columns sections, I can build a 15' x 24' structure, one which most armature astrono0mers only dream of.

I glanced at my spouse, busy reading a book on home decorating, and dared to ask, "What if I covered the roof opening above the kitchen, and build a real observatory to match our home?"

"A real observatory? But, Honey, don't you feel you had enough of building for a while?"

Her question valid, I gave her cautious glance, "To be truthful, I have, but this will be different: a more unique project for me. Sort of a reward for building our retirement home."

Anne managed a cute smile. "Our friends were right! I really married a workaholic."

Happy, I gave her quick hug. "Yes, a workaholic who built for you the most beautiful home on this mountaintop."

She hugged me back. "Yes, you did, and thank you."

I pulled back to show a grin. "Seetheart! Does that mean, yes?"

Anne's coy smile should have warned me. "I don't know why you had to ask," She replied. "You do what you want."

To see my Love her go back to reading her book, her response brought up for me a serious questions. Have I become a workaholic? Or have I always been one? What was it that drove me to such extremes? These questions and others are answered in the last chapter of this journal.

The preliminary drawings of the observatory completed, I gave them to John for his professional touch.

"That's some observatory, Dad. What kind of telescope are you planning?"

"I'm not sure. Maybe a 16-inch Cassegrain. However, this time, I'll not spend hours grinding the mirror. I'll order a ready-made."

I presented my drawings to the Riverside Building and Safety office for a plan check. The clerk saw how the observatory resembled our home, and grinned. "You're the couple who built a home, resembling a Greek temple."

"Guilty!" I said. Several weeks later a notice in the mail asked us to pick them up for additional calculation. It appeared the flat concrete roof structure and dome support needed a structural engineer to make it safe. Though I expected this, I was shocked later at the $600 fee, charged for a three hour job. No doubt this firm charged on a sliding scale. Sure, for an ordinary guy, the observatory structure looked impressive, but we could hardly be called rich.

Anne didn't miss my perturbed look, and had to tease, "Oh, the price we must pay for our adult toys."

To locate the observatory was quite easy on our three plus + acres. We placed it some distance from tall trees, and hills more than 30 degrees above the horizon. To avoid the Architectural committee's wrath, I placed it about 250 feet from the street, away from street lights.

No problem this time with the Committee's approval. We had our dozer operator shave off about two feet of dirt for the pad, to a natural grade of mixed decomposed granite for a more solid foundation.

Building the observatory was same as the home, except on a much smaller scale. The roof would be almost flat except for the dome support ring on the north end. I placed all the needed steel in the footings, and used #5 vertical bars, 16 inches on center for the masonry walls.

In the north half of the building, under the proposed dome, part of the concrete slab was isolated from the rest, by inserting a 2-by-6 lumber, 5-foot square. This would be removed after the pour to create an isolated pedestal for the telescope. With such isolation, the movement of the dome or slamming the door would not affect the quality of long photographic exposures of deep the sky.

After the building inspector's sign off, we ordered the ready mixed concrete for the footings, and slab. We made the pour without a hitch, as Jim skillfully finished the slab. To lay concrete blocks felt somehow different this time. This, being my own observatory, made it more a labor of love than a job that must be done on schedule. Every block I put down brought my star-gazing nights closer. Since I've been in this building process off and on for some time, the laying of blocks this time was a labor of love.

Though I began to count the months before retirement, five years seemed like forever, for me. In a way, staying busy was a blessing for us both. However, the aluminum dome with automatic powered shutters became a problem. To keep rain from moving parts was another. Despite all these challenges, the anticipation of a new instrument made this the project of my dreams.

Many times I felt a tinge of guilt leaving my wife alone in the house. I purposely created small jobs around our home to be with Anne. She sensed this, and scolded, "What are you doing here? Go and finish your beautiful observatory."

At times. I thought, this must be a sin, because no one deserves to be this happy. Doing what I liked best, I almost could see what heaven would be like, even wondered if the Good Lord allowed telescopes only for workaholics like me.

As my block-laying progressed, I made sure to insert electrical conduits. I also put the metal conduits to the telescope pier, and higher up to power the dome movements. And since I've always seen the observatory as a sanctuary, I brought underground power lines from the main house. To stay in touch with Anne, I installed an AC line communicator to the main house. Which proved, we are not willing to cut that umbilical cord to the outside world. All we sometimes want is the right to choose a moment of solitude, to be alone with our thoughts, and our Maker.

To brace the plywood forms for the roof before pouring concrete, proved to be our biggest challenge. I called my expert concrete man to check all the bracing. Jim examined all the bracing and grinned. "Dad! This is not going anywhere,"

"It's always better to over-design than be sorry,"

We stood at the entrance to see what now resembled a timber forest with all the bracing used to support the pouring of the concrete roof. Another serious challenge was to design forms and supports for the 11-foot diameter dome opening. To make this round form, two 1/4-inch by 6" exterior plywood was bent into a 11 foot diameter circle. Spaced 8" inches apart. I then placed the completed ring form on the dome opening.

We took every precaution to keep this ring form in position, by bracing the sides to retain a perfect circle. When the concrete set, we would bolt on top of this concrete ring a 1'4 steel plate x 1/4-inch thick, on which the dome casters would ride. As the dome turned, the shutter opening would cover different parts of the night sky.

My brother Bob, and wife Dee, visited us the previous summer. Their enthusiasm for our observatory was fervent enough to get them involved. Back at his plant, Bob manufactured the six parts of the steel ring in his machine shop, and had them shipped to us from Long Island.

Camera Obscura, and Sun Scope?

I read in *Amateur Telescope Making* about a device called Camera Obscura. We had once driven to Santa Monica beach to examine the setup of this unique instrument. Our mountaintop provided a sensational view of distant cities and valley below. One problem however, was the 6-foot-high dome to be on the north end of the observatory roof, which would obscure half of the view. I was intrigued enough by this optical instrument to provide an opening for it in the southeast part of the roof. A three-pound coffee can was nailed on the ceiling form to create a six-inch hole in the roof. Six feet away, I placed another coffee can for a future Sun telescope. Most everyone knows, the image of the sun cannot be observed without first protecting the eyes. The sun telescope uses a rotating optically flat mirror with a fixed refractor lens to project an image on a white screen. A much safer method for sun observation.

It is quite easy to provide for these little extras while under construction. The cost? Two coffee cans. Imagine trying to drill perfectly round six-inch holes, in a thick roof slab reinforced with steel bars. After all the preparations for these unique instruments, circumstances beyond my control, I never completed them. Perhaps someday, someone will mimic my enthusiasm and finish the Camera Odscura, and Sun Scope.

Homemade Dome

Just to think of making the aluminum dome made me a bit apprehensive. I've read in amateur journals that modified silo domes, seemed to work well for small observatories, and can be ordered from farm catalogs. This option did not appeal to this tinkerer and amateur astronomer; it was too easy. An alternative was to order a manufactured dome, complete with shutters and drives from a company back east. But the price to me seemed prohibitive. It had cost us only $1,500 for the observatory so far; I was not ready to spend nearly three times that on a ready-made dome.

Back to that wonderful amateur astronomer's bible, *Amateur Telescope Making*. This informative magazine showed all the details on this subject, and gave me the satisfaction of building my own.

When the 18-gauge aluminum sheets I ordered arrived, I cut them into fat triangles, and in a few days assembled a fairly good-looking dome. The tools: a good pair of tin snips, pliers, and a lot of patience. A curved wooden-form jig with a six-foot radius helped me to achieve the right shape.

I had ordered optics for a 16-inch, F-15 and F-4 Cassegrain-Newtonian telescope. Which required a parabolic 16" main mirror, and two 4" inch secondary's. One a round hyperbolic, the other, a flat diagonal for the primary focus of the Newtonian. A large cash deposit to a Long Beach optical company ensured a good optical system.

Much to my consternation, the company postponed delivery several times. My eagerness t of wanting to see, and try out the new telescope in this ideal location was unbearable. The largest telescope I ever had was an 8-inch Cassegrain. But it was near a city, where a night sky hindered deep sky observation.

There was an advantage to my waiting for the mirror: I completely reworked the Springfield mounting, added more features, and improved the dome shutters, to make the operation smoother. A reversible DC motor with a double pole, double throw switch and a DC power supply was installed to power the dome movements.

Sometimes we become careless hiding our indiscretions from our spouse, "Andrew, when will the mirror arrive?" Anne asked one day.

Looking surprised, I asked, "How did you know I ordered my mirror?"

"Easy! First, you'll soon be through with the observatory. Second, the past few days you've acted like the cat that swallowed a canary, while a man from an optical company asking if you would consider a thicker mirror, which is ready for shipping."

There's not much one can say when caught by the best. After all, a husband can hardly minimize$2,000 expenditure. I sheepishly replied, "Honey! I wanted to make sure we had the optics when the dome was finished,"

I later rewarded my loving wife, by building her a classic vanity, fit for a Queen.

Telescope and Mounting

In designing a telescope tube, we had several choices on how it would mount, and interact with sky observations. Since the telescope would be sheltered indoors, the tube I chose was of the open network type. Four 19-inch diameter circular rings were cut, from 3/16-inch flat aluminum stock. After the rings were filed and polished, I clamped them all together and drilled six 3/16-inch evenly spaced holes, for the threaded rods to form the telescope tube.

I then cut a half-inch inside diameter aluminum pipe for correct spacing of the rings through which I inserted threaded rods. After cross-bracing the assembled tube with six 9-gauge threaded wires, the tube assembly felt quite rigid.

I had always dreamed of owning a Porter Springfield telescope mounting. I had stood many a cold night on stools and small ladders trying to get a comfortable position near the eyepiece. But, to move to a different part of the sky, I often had to climb down, and again fight for that difficult to find comfortable position for viewing celestial objects.

Porter's design of the famous 200-inch Hale telescope is still hailed as unique by astronomers over the world. This genius fired up the imaginations of many amateurs with his support and his design of the now-famous Porter mounting. It allows an observer to sit comfortably in one position and search the heavens in easy comfort. The only part of you that moves are your hands to operate the small cranks that adjust declination, and right ascension. Porter thought, an observer should be comfortable while observing the heavens.

Since I'm not a machinist, or have machine-shop experience, I made this mounting with simple tools. My workshop for many years had only a small drill press, and homemade lathe, lacking most of the essentials a machine-shop lathe needed, such as automatic feeds and variable speeds. It did have an adjustable rest bar for the cutting tools I made from old dull files. I could cut circles, trim cylinders and put in delicate curves in an experimental metal mirror I had once made.

With the drill press and this lathe I made the mounting out of scrap 1/4-inch and 1/2-inch flat aluminum stock. I needed help with the declination shaft, its housing and bearing. Our good neighbor Harry Hodges took my sketch to his plant and had his machinist make it. Another one installed the brass bearing. We appreciated our small community of unique neighbors, who were a blessing to crazy hobbyists like me.

To make the adjustable mirror cell, I used aluminum to maintain a light assembly for easy tracking. Finally, all the assembled pieces fit together and were ready to mount on the precast concrete pier. I very carefully lowered the 16-inch Pyrex mirror into the cell and attached the three padded retaining clamps to hold it in place.

Next step was a spider mount for the secondary mirrors. This was figured for a certain distance from the primary. I designed the threaded adjusting rod a bit longer than needed in case the focus of the primary mirror was different than specified. I then carefully aligned the optics from instructions found in *Amateur Telescope Making.*

This became the most enjoyable phase in assembling my new toy. Will it work to my expectations? I'll know for sure as I try out the instrument on the stars.

That Glorious First Look

Thanks to our location, the night sky is near perfect for deep sky observation. Anyone can plan a star party and not worry about a cloudy sky. As a former city dweller, I was fascinated with the exceptional dark sky. A person can easily pick out Andromeda with the naked eye any summer night. We had to get accustomed to the Milky Way being so bright, making it hard difficult to locate constellations. Star maps are a necessity in most observations.

I opened the dome shutters before sunset to give the mirror time to settle down with the cooler night air. I could hardly wait till dark to see the stars, so I pointed an already visible Jupiter to see if the mirror would resolve the bands while still in its cooling stage. The image looked excellent, though the mirror was still adjusting to the cooler night. The sharply defined bands around the planet pulsated like neon rings. This told me the optics in our new telescope performed with impressive results. For the first time in my life I had the urge to photograph the heavens.

I flipped the secondary mirrors to try the image at the primary focus. Again the telescope was superior to anything I had tried before. To see the much wider field at Newtonian focus, was such a relief from the Cassegrain position. The disadvantage: climbing a ladder to reach the eyepiece. Later, at the Cassegrain focus, I saw a new challenge. We needed a special double eyepiece, so two people could watch at the same time, one I had once seen in a magazine.

I still remember that awe-inspiring night, taking turns with different focus eyepieces. Though Anne and I were on a high already, we regretted not having a bottle of champagne to celebrate the performance of my new instrument.

Next, to find data on the Camera Obscura; what a challenging project, as would a sun telescope next year, present a new insight into my hobby. Our plans for the orchard and vineyard were a must, and will be completed next spring.

Four more years, I retire. What am I saying? There are not enough hours in the day to do the various chores that we wanted to try. Our nights aren't long enough for both star gazing and sleeping. Perhaps in the next millennium, Earth will decelerate its rotation, just a little, creating longer days and nights to satisfy these resolute, middle-aged earthlings.

Stardust In Our Lives

If you enjoy a good night's sleep, astronomy is not for you. You will miss most of the asteroids and comets that often fly by our planet. Actually, it's better that way; because you'll be spared the cold fear of cataclysmic near-misses of our planet by these wanderers of the sky. A theory you read about two years ago is now obsolete, replaced with a new one, probably by a slip of a girl in a far-away university. You may hear of some Japanese high-school kids who had a comet named after them. This no doubt will go into the class Year Book, and *Astronomy and Astrophysics Abstracts journal*. Surely, *Sky and Telescope* magazine will have two pages on his discovery.

Should you want astronomy as a hobby, you must be well informed, and thoroughly involved in all aspects of this expansive field. Actually, the hobby may increase your chances of being the ideal Renaissance Man-Woman To maintain interest however, you must have a basic knowledge of optics and mathematical formulae that go with this high-tech hobby. How else can you grind and test your refractor lens, or mirror?

The amateur should also have a small machine shop and the training to use it. This allows you to build the special telescope tubes, mountings and lens cells that most astute amateurs always build, and write about.

As a dedicated amateur you will put your marriage to a true test by staying up half the night looking for a known or unknown heavenly object. If you discover it by chance, you will no doubt upset the old established astrophysics theories, which will carry your name. You will be famous, until a slip of a girl in a faraway university makes a new discovery and nullifies yours theory.

I do not regret my involvement in this fascinating hobby; I do however, bemoan the time it stole from my growing family. At times I acted as if entranced, working on these projects for hours without stopping to chat or dine with them. To explain my behavior to my loved ones was not easy. To me, astronomy was a most the intriguing and thought-provoking enterprise I've encountered.

The awesome feeling of vastness pervades one's thought while observing galaxies millions of light years away. We sometimes ask; what minute specks of insignificant nothings are we in this vast universe? Yet, without us as observers, would it matter if it existed at all? Is intelligent life absolutely necessary for the universe to be held in awe?

When finally we mentally grasp the vastness of space, and time while we observe these wondrous celestial objects, I am thoroughly convinced that one cannot be an egotist while immersed in this unique endeavor.

To avoid more future lonely nights for my loving spouse, I've considered joining a bird watcher's club. First however, I must find a way to enhance this fascinating new telescope. An electronic image intensifier or maybe an illuminated reticule guiding eyepiece would help. Be patient my devoted spouse, in 30 or 40 years I will tire of this illuminating pastime and once more become the loving, and caring person you married.

CHAPTER FOURTEEN

HOME COMPLETION

Because of my natural curiosity in many fields, I've read several how-to books on varied subjects, wondering why some authors do not expand on the emotional aspect of their projects, their feelings and possible impact their project may have on their family

As I began the last part of this journal, I asked myself, would my readers be interested in this final part of our building story? If so, how much of our private life must I disclose to achieve my purpose? Finally: shall I be frank or just finish with, "The happy retired couple strolled hand in hand into the colorful sunset."

After carefully weighing the need of this chapter, I decided an honest response to these queries would be best. In the introduction of this book, I pretty much a promised a step by step account of a middle-aged couple building their retirement home. Telling them why they did this in midlife, and the possible impact it would have on their life and marriage

On completion of our home, several friends asked if we had the desire to build another. Taken by surprise, I said, "Ask me a couple of years from now."

Not all of us will want to build that second home in our middle years. Many couples do not want the hassle of such a time-consuming endeavor. This less adventurous group will opt for a more stoic pre-retirement life. Such a fast-paced living environment has been their mainstay for many hectic years, as they tried to eke out a comfortable living. For these people, this would be the time to coast a little, gear down a bit, and enjoy the few years before retirement.

To be frank, building houses for a living would not be my choice. The building business has many facets, requiring much capital investment plus devotion to each project. A contractor without an excellent manager may devote 10 to 12 hours a day till the project is completed. This type of undertaking takes much dedication and no doubt will impact his personal life.

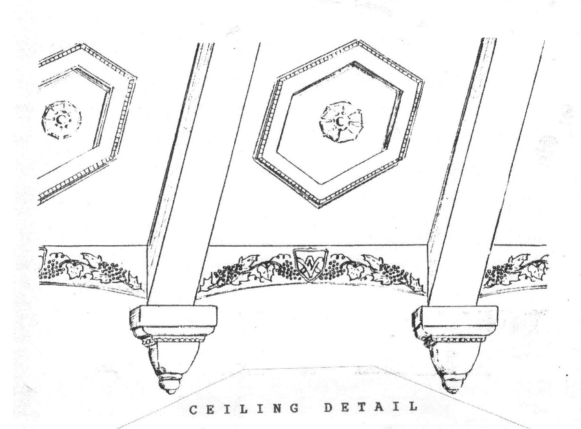

CEILING DETAIL

Showing Hexigon Frames With
Rossette and Stenciled Crown.

CROWN STENCIL

This does not apply to owner-builders, planning their dream home. Such a joint venture will not only involve husband and wife, but the whole family. They will spend more hours together than they have in a long time, sharing the same goal, a successful completion of their unique dwelling. The children's participation will unite more the family, but may act as an incentive to someday build their own. Yes, there is a different sense of involvement towards a house meant as a home, than toward one meant to be a speculation.

Several years ago we invested in a three-acre parcel with two small homes needing minor repairs. A young father in the main house enjoyed the country atmosphere so much, he asked that we enlarge it for his growing family. He would not mind a reasonable increase in rent. After a careful study of the floor plan, we decided to turn the living room into a den, and add a larger living room.

A curious phenomenon occurred after drawing plans and beginning the addition. We did not feel the same fire and zest, we had in building our first home. Surely, we thought, it would add to our income and increase the value of our investment. But, to leave my family to work on this rental was such a chore, my enthusiasm quickly dwindled. I couldn't wait till the job was completed so we could go on with our lives.

This was our last remodeling job of our rentals. We decided that the monetary reward was not a priority. If we needed to remodel in the future, we would hire someone, and for tax purposes, ad the cost to the value of the property.

There was a remarkably difference when we began to plan our second home. Our total time and effort did not appear as a sacrifice; rather a fast paced, and exhilarating moment in our quiet life.

If asked again about my desire to build another home, without hesitation I would say yes. As we grow older we need these stimuli to infuse meaning into our lives. Just to think about it now brings me the sensation of a pending adventure. The longing to redraw some of the old plans in the study, and manipulate the room locations on floor plans would be just the ticket to spice up my life. This time however, a smaller lot and a less prestigious abode would be considered. After all we did our big thing, we build a home to last a thousand years; how many couples can make such a claim.

With the low interest paid by banks, people should plan other strategies to increase retirement income. If you crave excitement in your life, now would be a chance to build a modest home with an extra suite mentioned in Chapter Five, and get more than 20-percent return on your hard-earned money. To make such profound decisions in midlife can be challenging, still the dividends of such a venture can be financially rewarding. When we see the many savings and loan banks going bottoms up, we should consider controlling our own funds with such sound moves. I have yet to see a prudent owner living in his duplex in financial trouble. Yet many elderly people have experienced trauma when they lost their life savings because some bank executive bought junk bonds with their money. For future retirees, home building with a curious and adventurous eye, I say, give it all you have as a farewell to those hard working, productive years. Though, I do not imply that we all build Mediterranean villas, all the building phases I described in building ours will apply for the one you choose. This could be a magnificent chance to not only make a mark in your retirement years, but fulfill dreams most have been nurturing. Since we only live our life once, we should make every effort to make the grand finale before aging renders us useless. Make your early retirement a Fourth of July ending. We should not dwell on negatives, musing on what could happen if we took a less challenging path to fulfill our dreams.

Many families will live out their lives in the same home, the same town that their great-grandparents enjoyed. I admire this trait of a family staying put, as it projects stability and permanence, implying their deep-rooted background in a historically stable community. I've read about many such staid families that live in New England states. I appreciate this simply because it is the complete opposite of my way of thinking and behavior.

In the past three decades we seldom lived more than twelve years at the same residence. Perhaps our ancestral bloodlines led to some remote Gypsy camp in central Europe. Or, maybe Asian Tartars that swept that central continent forced them to leave their homes for higher ground. Could this ancestral background have instilled in me this nomadic urge?

Thank God most of us are unique in our lifestyles and philosophies, else we would all be wondering nomads, scattering our tents in many nations across distant horizons.

Living in our unique mountaintop retreat has been for us a memorable experience, even though at times a mournful hoot of an owl woke us earlier than planned, the lack of coastal morning fog almost guaranteed a cheery sunrise every morning. Our unique location provided us a connection with nature undreamed of before. The tell-tale hoofprints by our reflection pond showed deer had made an occasional visit. An occasional site of a red-tailed hawk, soaring high in the sky is an exile rating site. One morning I got up earlier, and while making coffee, I had to suck in my breath on seeing a mountain lion perched on a rock, its magnificent head as if on a swivel as he searched the distant meadows for hs bearkfast, Hoping it would stay, I ran into our bedroom to wake my wife. Sleepy-eyed she complained, "To get up this early, this better be good."

In the kitchen I pointed, "Isn't he magnificent?"

Wide-eyed, she managed, "Yes! But not in my front yard."

To hike our community roads is an adventure in itself, as a red fox would dash to its young with food, while roadrunners made frenzied runs across the path. Yes, we often see pesky bee swarms, skipping kangaroo rats, and good and bad snakes. But so did the occupants of the legendary Garden of Eden. Our orchard and vineyard have matured beautifully providing us with fresh fruits, we sometimes sundry for the winter. We've experimented in winemaking with grapes, pears and plums. Some excellent, others mediocre; all added a bit of zest to our ranch activities.

The observatory was a blessing in a more unconventional way. A place to contemplate on life in a more somber vein, never quite sure that observing celestial objects is fun in the same sense as are other hobbies. I believe a spiritual aura envelops us while pursuing this engaging pastime. A solitude that does not compare with other activities. The hobby also introduced me to the exemplary art of meditation, giving me the ability to understand better the unique person into which I've grown. Though I never took part in serious scientific programs, I thoroughly enjoyed the observatory, and my celestial studies became a time of simple pleasure.

To say that our home and its unique location improved the quality of our life would be a understatement. A more befitting declaration would be, to have built our home on that mountaintop has fulfilled most of our retirement fantasies. If asked what we would change if we could do it again, my response would be "Very little. We enjoyed every step of our home-building adventure. We see it as a memorable highlight in our lives."

In my last walk among the grapevines to savor the ripeness of the fruit, a compelling urge to give thanks, overcame me. I thanked God for His guidance, as all this came at the most appropriate time in our lives.

Though we all hear a different drummer, I would not hesitate to advise most couples to build on that dream of a special home. Whether you do it yourself, or supervise others to build it, the reward will be there. Whatever gains you've experienced in the past will seem like a rehearsal to what you will feel as you move into your beautiful new home.

CHAPTER FIFTEEN

AUTHOR'S BIO— SUMMING UP

I found most of the self-help books were informative, but not a single one touched on the emotional and personal problems associated with one's project. Mine goes into detail of all the building phases, and how one can get carried away while building a dream home.

Let me first tell you a little about my life, and how my wife and I got involved in building our first home. Better yet, let me start, by telling you a little about my beginnings as a newcomer to America.

I was born in a two hundred year old oak-log home, in a little country of Slovakia. As the eldest of four boys, my weekly job was to sprinkle water on the dirt floor before sweeping. Our one large room was divided into two open sleeping areas, separated by a kitchen with a large iron stove.

Plumbing? We had none, even lacked electricity. A kerosene lamp was lit on nights we stayed up. Strange, we, didn't mind the hardship. While our vagabond Dad was away selling men's toiletries, Mom would take charge by trying on a stern face. But, we boys weren't scared. Compared to Dad, her spankings were love-taps,

Once every two weeks, we'd see Dad put on a blue pin-striped suit, gray spats, and snappy Hamburg hat. With a polished cane in hand, our neighbor said, Dad more resembled a Hungarian Count,

While Dad was away, our sweet Mom must have believed that morning exercise was beneficial. As the eldest, I was assigned the task of walking about 80 meters to the village well. I didn't mind the walk, but the two wooden pails were heavy, and at times I'd spill half of the water before I got home. My reward was the look in our milk cow's eyes, when I brought the water. Even more, when Mom made donuts, and I was put first in line.

On extra cold mornings, I'd feel sorry for our poor Mom, making breakfast, while her boys crowded around the kitchen stove. Our worst scenario however, occurred on a cold winter night, when our potty overflowed, and we had to walk some 15 meters in the snow to the outhouse.

This little place also became a problem in the summer: For years, the villagers used our front yard as a path to get to their homes. Naturally, their right of passage was irrevocable. We did not mind, except when we needed to use the little house. Imagine an eight year old boy about to go, and he sees pretty girls, coming up the path. I naturally kept walking toward an apple tree near the outhouse, pretending to pick apples.

Actually, we didn't really mind some of the difficulties, especially during school vacation. After our assigned chores, the four of us went to the river, and swim all day. Our river however, originated from nearby mountain, the reason for its pristine quality, but also was very swift. If one forgot, they'd soon get carried away to the deepest area, and had to swim like mad to get to shore.

I know because that happened to me. Unable to touch bottom, I became desperate, and swam like crazy, but the current kept taking me into deeper water. Lucky for me, a city lad heard me yelling, and went after me.

Afraid I'd pull him down; he kept pushing my head toward the shore. Each time he did, my head went under, causing me to swallow more river water. Lucky for me, our r water was the safest to drink. How odd that I forgot to thank that city lad for saving my life.

If asked what I missed about my little country, I'd say, my littlest brother, Rudy, who at age four, died of pneumonia on Christmas Eve. The other, I'd miss, are the summers I ran barefooted on the village green, chasing butterflies.

When I turned nine, our vagabond father lucked out when a countryman in America offered him a job. Two years later, our lonely Dad asked his employer to sign a document, so he could have us join him in a small steel town in Western Pennsylvania.

Happy could not describe what we felt as we boarded a train for Prague. More so in meeting an American consul, who seemed so pleasant, commenting on our haircuts. In Hamburg, we kids didn't even mind the Third class accommodations.

The boat trip in December however, was a bit rocky for mom, who became seasick. Six days later, seeing the Statue of Liberty was what made our day. And what a surprise to be treated like royalty by the Ellis Island people.

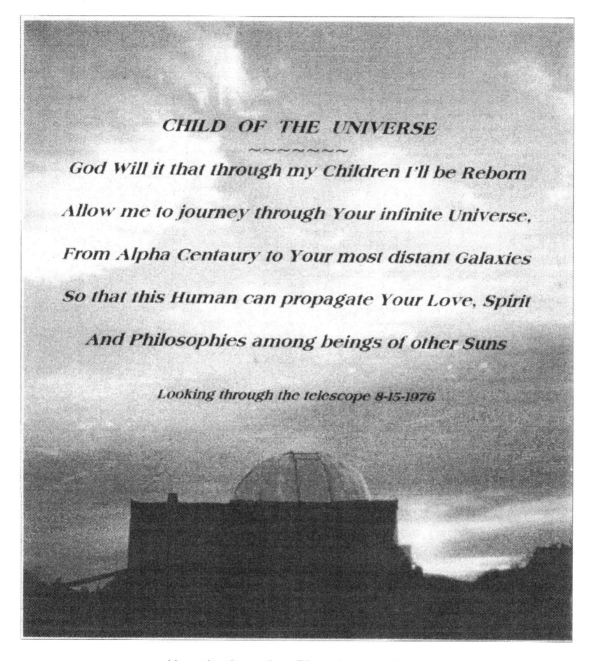

Verse by the author. Photo by John Salat

My best helper?
Anne Marrie

The Choice Of Paris	Woman With Vase	Allegory - Virtue
Sebestiano Ricci - 1634 - 1731	Unsigned 19th Century	L.T. Stiepenoff - 1854 - 1911

At 3000 ft .Elevetaion, our
pond turned into a Scating Ring

Jumping the Gun?
"Not really," said my happy woman. "Building a patio
on top of the wolrd, few could resist bringing up furniture."

A five hour train ride through the small hamlets of Pennsylvania were a joy to watch as they flit by. What a surprised to see Dad meet us at the station, take us to a white milk truck, and drive us to our first American home. When we arrived, Dad turned sad, saying, "I just remembered: Where is little Rudy?"

If worried before, Mom broke into tears. "Adam, I am sorry, but last Christmas, our little Rudy died of pneumonia."

"My God! Why didn't you tell me?"

With lumps in our throats, we waited for our tearful Mom, to speak. "I cried every night for months, wondering, how a mother could explain in a letter, a sweet child's death?

Took a while for Dad to hug her. "Not your fault."

Our first night in America could have been our last. I smelled something different in our bedroom, and complained, "What is it that smells so strong on our bedroom?"

Dad grins. "You'll soon get used to different smells."

Too much for this farm boy, I crawled under our bed, and hearing a hissing noise, saw the problem, and quickly yelled, "Dad, a pipe with no cap, is what smells."

Dad chased us outside, and called the, owner, A big mustached Russian arrived within minutes, and quickly capped the pipe. Finished, he looked us over. "Which one of you found the problem"

My brothers pointed at me. "Good boy! This could have been you last day in America."

Face drawn, Dad, without a word came to hug me, and I understood his silence. For months he had waited for us for three years, and nearly lost us.

Two years, later, Dad bought our first American home. Imagine our joy of moving into a three-bedroom, two indoor baths, and beveled glass French doors separated the dining room, from a spacious living room. Most impressive was a fancy ceramic fireplace.

The best part, we had a large back yard, where our Mom loved to plant vegetables, and a small orchard. We'd see her drop her boring house chores to lovingly pamper her tomato plants, or rescue her cabbage from caterpillars. For variety, the brilliant flower beds in the front yard, received her tender care, and soon won her the town's Beautification award.

Summer time, we kids lucked out in finding a wide river flowing by our steel town. Our pleasure was to catch the big waves, made by the boats pushing long coal barges.

However, unlike our river in Slovakia, this one had a terrible odor. If accidentally swallowed, it left an acidy taste in our mouths. Yes, we finally discovered our new country had flaws. But living in three bedrooms, with electricity, and indoor plumbing, we thought we were in Paradise.

Yes, it was tough for us learning a new language, especially degrading for me when instead of fifth grade, I was placed in third. A head taller than most kids, I'd slump down in my seat, so the teacher couldn't see me.

But once she did see me, and motioned to me, "Salat, I want to see you after class."

Worried, I wondered what I've done wrong. Class over, Miss Ready came over to where I sat, and asked, "Andrew, can you tell me your thoughts while gazing out the window?"

I dared to look into her dark eyes, "I remember now: At that time I imagined running barefooted through the village green, while chasing butterflies."

First an odd look, then a smile. "I see we have another Hemmingway in my class."

Not having heard of Hemmingway yet, I was told to go home. I don't know why, but afterward, Miss Ready, seldom failed to ask me about geography lessons.

My two brothers and I soon overcame our difficulties, even learned to play baseball. My crowning glory came in the playground, where I hit a home run, and had my new buddies congratulate me. First Hemmingway, and now Stan Musial Hey, I love America.

The countryman, who first hired Dad, also gave me my first job. Soon, I found another in a local bakery. One day I noticed several trucks idle in the parking lot, and went to see the big boss.

"Mr. Greenwald, I see several trucks without drivers. If you gave me one, I could start a retail route? You know? Sell house to house."

The older man looked me over, and grinned, "So my Greenhorn is tired of greasing pans, and wants to start a retail route. Good, but understand, it will take a lot effort to sell to housewives."

"I'm not worried," I said. "We have many Slavic friends; maybe I can convince some to buy bread, and pastry."

I not only got the job, but an unheard of five-Dollars a week raise. Soon I had customers waiting for my bread and donuts. At age twenty, I also met a girl from across the river, one I couldn't wait to see. Anne would be on the back porch looking out for my red bakery truck, then run out, waiting for me, a doorknob in her hand.

"Why the doorknob?" I asked grinning. "I know, you saw my red truck, and couldn't wait to see me."

Her freckled smile always made my heart race. "The landlord knows, but doesn't care."

At age sixteen, Anne was too young to be engaged, so Instead of a ring, I gave her a tiny gold watch. The engagement however, was short-lived because of Pearl Harbor. I received my citizenship papers on Monday, and on Wednesday, the local Draft board sent me a notice.

I had tried several times to join the Air Force, bat was denied because I lacked citizenship papers. Talking about fast communication: The Pittsburgh Courthouse, and our local Draft Board had to be the fastest.

Basic training at Indiantown Gap was a breeze. Our maneuvers near Jacksonville, Flarida, turned out to be a killer. Tired after running all day, we tried to cool off in a muddy river, only to see Water Moccasins swimming next to us, "You Yanks need not worry!" A lad from Georgia yelled. "They can't bite under water."

The one true thing I can say about the Army, we traveled in style on the Queen Mary. Though our staterooms had inlaid Mother-of-Pearl ceilings, we had share to them with about thirty guys.

Things improved in England, when we were billeted in the famous Tidsworth Barracks. The nice thing, about our weekends in London, and other historic places, they were paid by a very generous Uncle Sam. Our landing practices off Scotland however, were the toughest. When through, we boarded an English ship with a Hindu crew. Two days later, the ship's speakers announced we'd be invading a North African town of, Oran.

Partially occupied by Germans, the French Colonial pilots, strafing the beaches obviously tried to miss most us.

A month later, our train ride across Algeria to Tunisia was long and boring. Passed along were rumors, the Germans we were to engage, were seasoned Russian front veterans, sent here on a well deserved vacation. One morning we were asked to take a rocky ridge occupied by the enemy I never dreamed the Germans, were capable of such carefully prepared defense. strategies. To get to our objective, our company had to dash over a rocky ridge through a deadly ankle-grazing machine-gun fire. The bad part, we had to sidestep fallen Buddies. Those that made it, ended up in a gully, already zeroed in by enemy mortars.

I must have fallen asleep, while pounded by mortar shells, until that evening. When I woke up, I asked my Sergeant about our losses. Eyes like saucers, he stammers, "With . . . your jacked smoking, we . . . we thought you were one of them."

"About our losses," I repeated. He gave me a hard look, but stayed silent.

We lucked after that battle by finding an oasis with hot Roman baths. Our memories short, everyone undressed and splashed around for hours.

I was later wounded, in another battle, and assigned to a Guard Company. Now, that I'm older and wiser, I believe the human mind is a paradox: After our heavy losses, not a single soldier shed a tear for a lost buddy. Now, 65 years later, long after the passing of my loving Anne, I see a young mother usher her three children into van, and reminded of my young family, I suddenly can't stop my tears.

After three long years, I was sent home, and talked my girl into marriage. So overjoyed were my parents, they paid for the biggest wedding, with an eight piece Polka band. With most young men still in the service, I used most of the evening driving our guest home. When finished, I found my kid sister by my sleeping bride, and scolded, "Why didn't take her to the spare room?"

Her freckled smile spoke volumes. "I wanted to, but Anne looked so beautiful in the moonlight, I didn't want to leave her."

I gathered my beautiful bride into my arms, and carried her up a flight of stairs, where I met Dad, who had to tease, "I hope you two aren't too tired."

"Go to bed, Dad." I scold."

As I close the door behind me, my bride opens her beautiful eyes, and smiles/ "That's no way to treat a man, who just paid for our wedding?"

Tired, I shake my head, "You too?"

With only days before my leave is over, I asked my bride to wait until I find a place by the camp, before she came to join me.

She breaks out in tears, "You're going on our honeymoon without me?"

"But, finding an apartment in a military town is next to impossible."

"I don't care. I want to be with you."

"Sweetheart, I just bought a used car, and hotels rooms are expensive."

She asked with a wide-eyed look. "How expensive?"

"About thirty-five dollars a day."

"I have enough money for five days,"

"Sorry! I need more time."

Assigned to a barracks, at camp Wheeler, I asked a noncom about renting an apartment.

"Forget apartments. You'll probably end up in a converted chicken-coop."

I thought he was kidding. A week later, I call my bride, to tell her, I found on almond orchard on the outskirts of Macon, renting of all things, a converted chicken-coop."

"I don't care. Meet me at the station, tomorrow night."

I'm at the Macon train station, waiting for my girl. When she finally arrives, I get a hesitant hug, and a sad look. "Sorry! It's that time of the month."

"So what? It's not the end of the world."

I get another hug, along with a sweet smile. "Always loved you for your sharp mind."

Living at the almond ranch was not that bad, except on Sunday morning, a loud calliope playing religious songs awakened us. That was the first Sunday we made it to the first Mass.

The other advantages of living on an almond ranch; my freckled-faced bride usually stuffed her pockets with almonds, thus saving us grocery money.

We soon found an apartment, only to discover our neighbors were musical people, the wildest bunch we ever met. Anne told our priest, who obliged by coming to bless our place. As if by magic, we soon were alone, as all the wild ones moved away.

In the summer of 1945, Germany finally surrendered, and all the Citizen soldiers were sent home. Our good fortune, my folks owned a three story triplex, and let us have a cute little apartment on the third floor, Anne called Heaven.

All the stories you may have heard about in-laws are false: Anne so loved my mother, she soon learned the Slovak language so they could communicate better. Mom in return, taught her to cook Slavic dishes, sewing, and best of all, gardening.

Dad managed to get me a high-paying job at the steel mill, but I was unhappy. I had read about a fairyland called, California, where many war veterans settled, and that's what I wanted.

Dad looked stunned. "But Son, you get paid by tonnage, about the best job in the mill. Why do you want to go to California, and start over again?"

"All you said is true," I replied, "But I've seen the world, but never a smoky town like this. Since Anne is with our first child, we don't want to raise it in this smoky town."

I recall the morning we loaded our prewar Chevy with our belongings, and Mom's tearful face. Guilt-ridden, I hugged her, "I promise this: Every three years, we'll come and see you, and bring the kids."

I found it tough in los Angele, attending classes at the famous Art Center School, while working evenings at a UPS facility. After Anne miscarried our first child, she got a waitress job. The prettiest waitress waiting on the school staff, soon was offered a modeling job, and we had it easier.

I never received my diploma, because Anne soon became pregnant. Since we didn't want our child to live in a rooming house, we began to look for a home. To our surprise, with the GI's Bill, we could buy a home for under $10,000, with only $300 down, and payment of $48 a month including taxes.

Our home however was tiny, and in the city. As a former country boy, I wanted to live in a semi-rural area. Anne gives me a surprised look, "But, Honey, we're doing well in Downey. Why do you want to move?" I thought staying mum was best.

Readers, please note the following, regarding economic conditions, and building lots.

The postwar years in California were fast paced even for our lively spirits, as many war industries converted to auto and household goods. A second economic boost came when the Russians launched the first Sputnik satellite, prompting many start-ups in high-tech aerospace industries. Swamped with demands for physicists, electronic engineers, and specialized technicians, many universities changed curriculums to fill this vacuum.

In this unprecedented growth, land developers were the biggest winners as new housing tracts spread, giving veterans a chance at the American dream. Anne and I were amazed when told that our $900 savings qualified us as home buyers.

Southern California with its expanding population was the perfect setting for prudent real-estate investors. A place for war veterans, where hopes were renewed and dreams became a reality. One could buy a home with a small down, rent it out to meet payments, and sell when prices rose.

This was not our method. We saw larger lots close in town with a growth potential faster than that of outlying areas. We bought large city lots with improvements, rented them for income until the area built up enough to cause rezoning, and a rise in value.

One Sunday after church, a real-estate ad showing a small house on an acre avocado grove, with sixty avocados and citrus trees, with an unbelievable low price. When the broker showed us the house: a 600 square foot cabin, which appeared to be built overnight, I wrote him a check for, (Baby-boomers take notice), $11,000.

We later found, this little town had great real-estate bargains for the beach folks of southern California. The hills above were a place to build an inexpensive weekend cottage, as an escape from the fast moving crowds of the coast. The exterior walls were of single vertical board and batten, with no studs, once called a "California house." After I solemnly promised my young family, I would build a larger home on an adjoining hill. all sighed with relief.

Plans for house drawn, one morning a grading contractor wanted to see the building site. The three of us climbed the hill to the top, and stopped. Below, we could see many small towns, and beyond the big ships in Long Beach harbor. What took our breath away, gleaming in the blue Pacific was the Dance Pavilion of Catalina Island.

Amazed, Anne and looked at each other; I'm tongue-tied, she spoke first, "Why build an ordinary house, on a lot with a Million-Dollar view?"

I agreed, and quickly redrew the plans, ending up with multi storied, 2,700 Sq. Ft. mansion, with three bedrooms, three baths, two fireplaces, and on the third floor, an observatory.

Our excitement nearly boiled over after the plans were drawn. It seemed we never had enough information about building materials, and home decoration. After a couple of teetering decisions, we chose a design that meshed with the style of our neighborhood homes. A combination of ranch and contemporary. I made the entire first floor, a large family room, a laundry with bath, and a two car garage Kitchen, living room, and sleeping areas were on the second floor, and the single room on the third floor would be the observatory.

Our ten blessed years in our owner built home, provided our children with pleasant memories of growing up in a semirural area. With a touch of guilt as a busy father, I would take time to build go-carts with my sons, and tried the precarious little vehicles on our long driveway. Joan, our daughter needed a stable for her mare, Tammy. Though the corral was designed by a now experienced home builder, this animal often escaped by nudging the wood dowel with her nose, thus releasing the gate's hasp.

One morning a neighbor's phone call shook us up. "Andrew, guess who I see feasting on our lovely green lawn? Tammy and her foal."

A three-step lock on her gate finally baffled our canny mare.

Looking back, brings many memories, so important in our lives. Though we counted our blessings, human nature is such that we are not fully aware of our good fortune. I suppose, being young and ambitious we search for impossible goals, thus lose ourselves in not seeing the forest for the trees.

Oddly, we sometimes felt there were parts of us everywhere we had lived, but unlike the pigeons, our homing instinct didn't exist. Our eleven-year stay at our lovely home ended when we found our building site, sold our home, and bought a duplex in San Juan Capistrano. The move brought us within 27 miles of our future weekend retreat.

That first summer of construction, my sister Ronnie and Mother decided on a two-week California visit. I can happily say, their visit was a welcome break for us. I recall their first night at our unfinished mountain retreat, and Ronnie's comment: "My brother is the only man I know who has bats in the belfry."

I looked up at the little furry mammals fluttering among the rafters. "They're not that dangerous. Most stories you hear about bats are fables.".

"Just the same, I wish this house had windows. Bats scare me."

Anne ad to but in. "I guess we've all seen too many Bella Lugosi movies, And, by the way Ronnie, I never asked how you slept last night?"

"You won't be offended?"

"I know. Our thrift store mattress is lumpy."

I recall after two nights, Ronnie and Mother had enough, and preferred the luxury of our townhouse in San Juan Capistrano.

A haunting occurrence for me was a trip to Long Beach to show our guests the luxury liner, *Queen Mary*, a ship that took my First Infantry division to England. Walking the decks, my heart went out to the families of my Buddies, who never returned.

A year later, we moved into our beautiful home on Thanksgiving week. On that memorable holiday the entire family celebrated the near-completion of our home. Though the place needed stucco, and decorating touches, our dream became a reality as each contributed his share to our new beginnings on that lovely mountain.

That Thanksgiving holiday was what caused us to sell our San Juan Capistrano duplex. and move permanently into our family retreat. The decision also enhanced our finances, as appreciating real-estate holdings would make our mature years more secure.

While shopping for a Christmas tree, Anne had to tease, "I can see our first Christmas tree will be limited by the height of our ceiling."

"Please don't make me buy a sixteen foot tree," I said. "Think of the fire hazard?"

Anne spoke of the traditional *kolachi* she planned to bake, hoping for a snow-fall to make it a perfect Christmas family holiday.

In a happy wishing mood, Anne gave me her famous smile. "And, after Christmas, what about a Valentine Day party for our new neighbors?"

Most of our property holdings were larger lots with improvements, which brought us extra income. My plan was to devote as much time as possible making our new home more comfortable. To get funds quickly, we put two properties on a slow market, sold one before, and the other after New Years to ease the capital-gains tax. This gave us a feeling of solvency, allowing us to finish decorating our home.

Our Crystal Ball however, must have malfunctioned, because the following year, property values in the Whittier area nearly doubled, This for us however, was inconsequential because we received double the value in peace of mind.

Anne seldom needed an excuse to throw a party. For our Thirtieth Anniversary, we invited many friends to help us celebrate, some drove hundreds of mile to be with us. We wanted this to be a memorable day, an affirmation of an exciting life we lived as two people best could.

One of our guests stood to speak, "To what do you attribute your long marriage?"

"There are several reasons for our successful marriage," Anne replied. "But boredom wasn't one of them.".

There was more wisdom in her words than intended. Perhaps we moderns should reassess our thinking, by placing more value on a higher level of a spiritual, rather than purely physical approach to a marriage. I often wonder about all those bridges we build as husband and wife: Are they meant to bring us closer together, or make an easy escape from each other at the first serious quarrel?

Some years ago our parents had asked that I not leave my high-paying job to go to California. We gave in to an adventurous spirit and went our way. Though our California beginnings were a bit shaky, our happy-go-lucky attitude usually made events happen to our advantage.

The little town we left however, suffered from a deadly smog attack, to where lives were lost, causing the factories to close. An event where Time magazine featured the story.

We had planted trees soon after we bought our land, so landscaping was not a problem. The cedar we put in as a seedling, now towered over the roof, competing with the graceful weeping willow by the colonnaded porch. All we needed was a small lawn in the front, and low sprawling junipers to accent the entrance steps. To add color, we put in African daisies as ground cover. What a surprise we had that winter on seeing the blossoms peek out of snow

The spring, after we moved into our home, with Anne's flower and vegetable garden, and my orchard blooming, we had the most colorful property in our community.

"I think I made a mistake in buying all these trees," I remarked one day. "What will we do with do with all the fruit?"

"The only mistake," Anne said. "you didn't plant enough. Remember, we have children and grand-children, and we can make fruit wines too."

We needed long ditches dug for the irrigation lines in our future orchard. How lucky for us to have neighbors who owned a rental company. Bud and Doris must have envisioned our colorful blooming orchard in front of their new home, and without hesitation, brought up a Ditch-Witch, to dig our irrigation trenches.

We put in nectarines, peaches, plums, and apricots. "No mini-ranch should be without nut trees." A friend advised. We planted ten almond trees.

Our reward was a fiery blossoming of the orchard the next spring. From the delicate waxy white of the almond, and apricot, to warmer hues of peach, and a shocking pink of nectarine.

After we bought our lot, a doctor of Italian descent advised us to plant an olive tree to signify peace. We definitely wanted peace in our home, so planted nine along the driveway."

The east end of our property had a slight grade away from the observatory, which according to a book on viticulture, an ideal place for a vineyard. We put in grape stakes for 250 vines, and strung wire to support them, and the irrigation lines.

My persevering spouse started a small vegetable garden, where she lovingly tilled around her young plants, sometimes speaking gently to them, or scolding the fast-growing weeds.

Anne's rose garden however, became her pride and joy. Joan, our daughter gave her a book on care and breeding of roses. The subject of breeding new hybrids came up in our conversation as a mysterious process to be tried by my avid rose lover.

Every spring, Anne's irises, and ranunculus exploded in surprising places, astounding my busy gardener. "Did I plant these bulbs last year, or was it the year before?" Anne would ask.

My observatory with a research grade telescope was not only a blessing, but escape from worldly problems. Our joy however, were our vineyard, orchard, and vegetable garden, making us feel as if we lived in a virtual Paradise.

My sincere wish, for my readers who plan to build their own home, they experience the same joy we have in building ours.

Good Luck.